International Labour and Employment Compliance Handbook

www.kluwerlawonline.com

Labour and Employment Compliance in Ireland

International Bar Association

Labour and Employment Compliance in Ireland

Ninth Edition

Duncan Inverarity

Tríona Sugrue

This publication is part of the International Labour and Employment Compliance Handbook, available on www.kluwerlawonline.com

Editors: Salvador del Rey and Robert J. Mignin
Associate Editor: Juan Bonilla

INTERNATIONAL BAR ASSOCIATION
the global voice of the legal profession

Wolters Kluwer

Published by:
Kluwer Law International B.V.
PO Box 316
2400 AH Alphen aan den Rijn
The Netherlands
E-mail: lrs-sales@wolterskluwer.com
Website: www.wolterskluwer.com/en/solutions/kluwerlawinternational

Sold and distributed by:
Wolters Kluwer Legal & Regulatory U.S.
7201 McKinney Circle
Frederick, MD 21704
United States of America
E-mail: customer.service@wolterskluwer.com

ISBN 978-94-035-0326-4

e-Book: ISBN 978-94-035-0636-4
web-PDF: ISBN 978-94-035-0646-3

All listed titles are also available on lrus.wolterskluwer.com

1. Argentina: Julio César Stefanoni Zani & Enrique Alfredo Betemps, *Labour and Employment Compliance in Argentina, 10th edition*, 2022 (ISBN 978-94-035-4332-1)
2. Australia: John Tuck, Stephen Price, Rosemary Roach, Jack de Flamingh, Nicholas Ellery & Nick Le Mare, *Labour and Employment Compliance in Australia, 6th edition*, 2021 (ISBN 978-94-035-3914-0)
3. Belgium: Chris Van Olmen, *Labour and Employment Compliance in Belgium, 7th edition*, 2022 (ISBN 978-94-035-4374-1)
4. Brazil: Rodrigo Seizo Takano, Andrea Giamondo Massei & Murilo Caldeira Germiniani, *Labour and Employment Compliance in Brazil, 9th edition*, 2022 (ISBN 978-94-035-4991-0)
5. Canada: Kevin Coon & Adrian Ishak, *Labour and Employment Compliance in Canada, 2nd edition*, 2014 (ISBN 978-90-411-5637-2)
6. Chile: Gerardo Otero A., María Dolores Echeverría F., María de los Ángeles Fernández S. & Javier Sabido, *Labour and Employment Compliance in Chile, 10th edition*, 2022 (ISBN 978-94-035-4404-5)
7. China: King & Wood Mallesons, *Labour and Employment Compliance in China, 6th edition*, 2021 (ISBN 978-94-035-3894-5)
8. France: Pascale Lagesse, *Labour and Employment Compliance in France, 10th edition*, 2022 (ISBN 978-94-035-4384-0)
9. Germany: Gerlind Wisskirchen & Martin Lützeler, *Labour and Employment Compliance in Germany, 10th edition*, 2022 (ISBN 978-94-035-4454-0)
10. India: Manishi Pathak, *Labour and Employment Compliance in India, 10th edition*, 2022 (ISBN 978-94-035-4362-8)
11. Ireland: Duncan Inverarity & Ailbhe Dennehy, *Labour and Employment Compliance in Ireland, 9th edition*, 2022 (ISBN 978-94-035-0326-4)
12. Israel: Pnina Broder-Manor, Helen Raziel & Ilan Winder, *Labour and Employment Compliance in Israel, 9th edition*, 2022 (ISBN 978-94-035-4424-3)
13. Italy: Angelo Zambelli, *Labour and Employment Compliance in Italy, 10th edition*, 2022 (ISBN 978-94-035-4372-7)
14. Japan: Yoshikazu Sugino, *Labour and Employment Compliance in Japan, 10th edition*, 2022 (ISBN 978-94-035-4342-0)
15. Republic of Korea: Sang Wook Cho, Soojung Lee & Christopher Mandel, *Labour and Employment Compliance in the Republic of Korea, 8th edition*, 2022 (ISBN 978-94-035-4434-2)
16. Mexico: Oscar De La Vega Gómez, *Labour and Employment Compliance in Mexico, 10th edition*, 2022 (ISBN 978-94-035-4414-4)
17. The Netherlands: Els de Wind & Cara Pronk, *Labour and Employment Compliance in the Netherlands, 5th edition*, 2022 (ISBN 978-94-035-1594-6)
18. Poland: Barbara Jóźwik, *Labour and Employment Compliance in Poland, 10th edition*, 2022 (ISBN 978-94-035-0316-5)
19. Russia: Anna-Stefaniya Chepik, *Labour and Employment Compliance in Russia*, 2013 (ISBN 978-90-411-4925-1)

20. Saudi Arabia: Sara Khoja & Sarit Thomas, *Labour and Employment Compliance in Saudi Arabia, 5th edition,* 2022 (ISBN 978-94-035-4394-9)
21. South Africa: Susan Stelzner, Stuart Harrison, Brian Patterson & Zahida Ebrahim, *Labour and Employment Compliance in South Africa, 10th edition,* 2022 (ISBN 978-94-035-4474-8)
22. Spain: Salvador del Rey, Ana Campos & Sergi Gálvez Duran, *Labour and Employment Compliance in Spain, 10th edition*, 2022 (978-94-035-4352-9)
23. Turkey: Sertaç Kökenek & Elif Nur Çakır Vurgun, *Labour and Employment Compliance in Turkey, 8th edition*, 2022 (ISBN 978-94-035-0336-3)
24. United Arab Emirates: Sara Khoja & Sarit Thomas, *Labour and Employment Compliance in the United Arab Emirates, 9th edition*, 2022 (ISBN 978-94-035-4444-1)
25. United Kingdom: Ed Mills, Ailie Murray, Anna West, Gareth Walls, Emmie Ellison & Elliot English, *Labour and Employment Compliance in The United Kingdom, 3rd edition*, 2022 (ISBN 978-94-035-4464-9)
26. United States: Andrew J. Boling, Amy de La Lama, William Dugan, Chris Guldberg, Brian Hengesbaugh, Robert J. Mignin, Virginia Mohr, John M. Murphy & Ginger Partee, *Labour and Employment Compliance in the United States, 7th edition*, 2022 (ISBN 978-94-035-3921-8)

International Bar Association
The Global Voice of the Legal Profession

The International Bar Association (IBA), established in 1947, is the world's leading organization of international legal practitioners, bar associations and law societies. The IBA influences the development of international law reform and shapes the future of the legal profession throughout the world. It has a membership of over 40,000 individual lawyers and almost 200 bar associations and law societies spanning all continents. It has considerable expertise in providing assistance to the global legal community.

Grouped into two divisions – the Legal Practice Division and the Public and Professional Interest Division – the IBA covers all practice areas and professional interests, providing members with access to leading experts and up-to-date information. Through the various committees of the divisions, the IBA enables an interchange of information and views among its members as to laws, practices and professional responsibilities relating to the practice of business law around the globe. Additionally, the IBA's high-quality publications and world-class conferences provide unrivalled professional development and network-building opportunities for international legal practitioners and professional associates.

The IBA's Bar Issues Commission provides an invaluable forum for IBA member organisations to discuss all matters relating to law at an international level.

The IBA's Human Rights Institute (IBAHRI) works across the Association, to promote, protect and enforce human rights under a just rule of law, and to preserve the independence of the judiciary and the legal profession worldwide.

Other institutions established by the IBA include the Southern Africa Litigation Centre and the International Legal Assistance Consortium.

Employment and Industrial Relations Law Committee

The aims of the committee are to develop and exchange knowledge of employment and industrial relations law and practice. Members support each other through the provision of innovative ideas and practical assistance on day-to-day issues. In addition, through its journal and through presentations, conferences, the committee ensures the dissemination of up-to-date law and practice in this highly important business area.

International Bar Association Global Employment Institute

The IBA Global Employment Institute (IBA GEI) was formed in early 2010 for the purpose of developing for multinationals and worldwide institutions a global and strategic approach to the key legal issues in the human resources and human capital fields.

Drawing on the resources and expertise of the IBA membership, the IBA GEI will provide a unique contribution in the field of employment, discrimination and immigration law, on a diverse range of global issues, to private and public organizations throughout the world. The IBA GEI is designed to enhance the management, performance and productivity of these organizations and help achieve best practice in their human capital and management functions from a strategic perspective.

The IBA GEI will become the leading voice and authority on global HR issues by virtue of having a number of the world's leading labour and employment practitioners in its ranks, and the support and resource of the world's largest association of international lawyers.

Further information

International Bar Association, 4th Floor, 10 St Bride Street, London EC4A 4AD, United Kingdom, Tel: +44 (0)20 7842 0090, Fax: +44 (0)20 7842 0091, E-mail: member@int-bar.org, www.ibanet.org

About the International Labour and Employment Compliance Handbook

From 1976 through 1988, the International Bar Association and Kluwer Law International published the groundbreaking International Handbook on Contracts of Employment. This Handbook provided one of the first global overviews of the law of the international employment relationship.

Since publishing the first edition, globalization of business has created an increased demand for knowledge of labor and employment laws throughout the world. Therefore, along with Kluwer, we decided to publish an updated Handbook which we have titled the International Labour and Employment Compliance Handbook.

This new Handbook was intended to be a practical guide by providing a general overview of key labor and employment issues in multiple jurisdictions. Each chapter was written so that it is easy to understand by lawyers and non-lawyers alike. Each country author has also followed a standard outline to assist readers in analysing employment issues in each country.

The first edition of this new Handbook included nineteen (19) different countries.

This Handbook would not have been possible without the help and assistance of many people. Most importantly, the individual country authors are all distinguished legal practitioners who spent considerable time drafting and revising their country reports to meet difficult deadlines. We thank each of them. Our friends at Kluwer, especially Ewa Szkatula, have done a wonderful job in keeping the editors and the authors on schedule. Finally, we want to also express our gratitude to Cuatrecasas, Gonçalves Pereira, and Baker & McKenzie LLP for their valuable assistance in the coordination and organization of this project. Our warmest thanks to each of them.

Because of the success of the Handbook,Wolters Kluwer Law & Business decided to publish each country report also as a separate book to give a choice in obtaining the information. We hope this new format will be a helpful and useful resource just like the Handbook. Both formats are available in print and online.

The Editors

Salvador del Rey Guanter
Robert J. Mignin

March 2013

Table of Contents

Authors ix

Legal Compliance in Ireland 1

1. Legal Framework: Employment Laws 1

2. Contracts of Employment 2

2.1. Overview 2
2.2. Written Employment Contracts 3
2.3. Oral Contracts 5
2.4. Employee Handbooks 5
2.5. Job Descriptions 5
2.6. Offer Letters 6
2.7. Checklist of Dos and Don'ts 6

3. Recruiting, Interviewing, Screening and Hiring Employees 6

3.1. Overview 6
3.2. Recruiting 6
3.3. Employment Applications 7
3.4. Pre-employment Inquiries 7
3.5. Pre-employment Tests and Examinations 8
3.6. Background, Reference, and Credit Checks 8
3.7. The Criminal Justice (Spent Convictions and Certain Disclosures) Act 2016 9
3.8. Interviewing 10
3.9. Hiring Procedures 10
3.10. Fines and Penalties 10
3.11. Checklist of Dos and Don'ts 10

4. Managing Performance/Conduct 11

4.1. Overview 11
4.2. Coaching and Counselling 11

4.3. Written Evaluations 11
4.4. Warnings and Suspensions 11
4.5. Checklist of Dos and Don'ts 12

5. Termination of Employees for Performance or Disciplinary Reasons 12
5.1. Overview 12
5.2. Separation/Severance Pay 13
5.3. Fines and Penalties 13
5.4. Checklist of Dos and Don'ts 13

6. Layoffs, Reductions in Force and/or Redundancies as a Result of Job Eliminations or Other Restructuring 14
6.1. Overview 14
6.2. Reductions in Force/Layoffs/Job Eliminations 14
6.3. Collective Redundancies 16
6.4. Fines and Penalties 17
6.5. Checklist of Dos and Don'ts 17

7. Labour and Employment Law Ramifications upon Acquisition or Sale of a Business 18
7.1. Overview 18
7.2. Acquisition of a Business 19
7.3. Acquisition Checklist 20
7.4. Sale of a Business 20
7.5. Sale Checklist 22

8. Use of Alternative Workforces: Independent Contractors, Contract Employees and Temporary or Leased Workers 22
8.1. Overview 22
8.2. Independent Contractors 22
8.3. Contract Workers/Fixed-Term Contract 24
8.4. Leased Workers 27
8.5. Checklist of Dos and Don'ts 28

9. Obligation to Bargain Collectively with Trade Unions: Employees' Right to Strike and a Company's Right to Continue Business Operations 28
9.1. Overview of Union's Right to Organize 28
9.2. Right of Employees to Join Unions 30
9.3. How Employees Select Unions 30
9.4. Pre-election Campaigning 30
9.5. Unfair Labour Practices 30
9.6. Relocation of Work/Shutdown of Business 31
9.7. Checklist of Dos and Don'ts 32

10. Working Conditions: Hours of Work and Payment of Wages: By Statute or Collective Agreements 32
10.1. Overview of Wage and Hours Laws 32
10.2. Hours of Work 32
10.3. Minimum Wage 33
10.4. Overtime 33
10.5. Meal and Rest Periods 33
10.6. Deductions from Wages 35
10.7. Exemptions to Wage and Hour Laws 35
10.8. Recordkeeping Requirements 37
10.8.1. Information That Must Be Maintained 37
10.8.2. Records That Must Be Retained 38
10.8.3. Failure to Maintain Required Records 39
10.9. Reductions in Compensation Caused by Economic Downturn 39
10.10. Checklist of Dos and Don'ts 39

11. Other Working Conditions and Benefits: By Statute, Collective Agreements or Company Policy 40
11.1. Health and Other Insurance 40
11.2. Pension and Retirement Benefits 40
11.3. Vacation and Holiday Payments on Termination 40
11.4. Leaves of Absence 41
11.4.1. Personal Leave 41
11.4.2. Medical or Sick Leave 41
11.4.3. Bereavement Leave 42
11.4.4. Family Leave 42
11.4.5. Pregnancy Leave 43
11.4.6. Maternity Leave 43
11.4.7. Injury at Work 45
11.5. Checklist of Dos and Don'ts 45

12. Workers' Compensation 45
12.1. Overview 45
12.2. Checklist of Dos and Don'ts 46

13. Company's Obligation to Provide Safe and Healthy Workplace 46
13.1. Overview of Safety and Environmental Laws and Regulations 46
13.2. Requirements 46
13.3. Rights of Employees 47
13.4. Rights of Employer 47
13.5. Specific Standards 47
13.6. Injury or Accident at Work 48

13.7. Workplace Violence 48
13.8. Fines and Penalties 48
13.9. Checklists of Dos and Don'ts 48

14. Immigration, Secondment and Foreign Assignment 49
14.1. Overview Laws Controlling Immigration 49
14.2. Recruiting, Screening and Hiring Process 49
14.3. Obligations of Employer to Enforce Immigration Laws 50
14.4. Fines and Penalties 51
14.5. Secondment/Foreign Assignment 51
14.6. Checklist of Dos and Don'ts 51

15. Restrictive Covenants and Protection of Trade Secrets and Confidential Information 52
15.1. Overview 52
15.2. The Law of Trade Secrets 52
15.3. Restrictive Covenants and Non-compete Agreements 52
15.4. Protection of Trade Secrets Regulations 53
15.5. Checklist of Dos and Don'ts 53

16. Protection of Whistle-Blowing Claims 54
16.1. Overview 54
16.1.1. Internal Disclosure to an Employer or Other Responsible Person 54
16.1.2. Disclosure to a Prescribed Person 55
16.1.3. Minister 55
16.1.4. Legal Advisor 55
16.1.5. Other Disclosures 55
16.2. Checklist of Dos and Don'ts 57

17. Prohibition of Discrimination in the Workplace 57
17.1. Overview of Anti-discrimination Laws 57
17.2. Age Discrimination 58
17.3. Race Discrimination 59
17.4. Sex Discrimination/Sexual Harassment 59
17.5. Handicap and Disability Discrimination 61
17.6. National Origin Discrimination 62
17.7. Religious Discrimination 62
17.8. Military Status Discrimination 62
17.9. Pregnancy Discrimination 62
17.10. Marital Status Discrimination 62
17.11. Sexual Orientation Discrimination 63
17.12. Retaliation 63

17.13. Constructive Discharge 63
17.14. Checklist of Dos and Don'ts 63

18. Smoking in the Workplace 64
18.1. Overview 64
18.2. Checklist of Dos and Don'ts 64

19. Use of Drugs and Alcohol in the Workplace 64
19.1. Overview 64
19.2. Checklist of Dos and Don'ts 65

20. AIDS, HIV, SARS, Blood-Borne Pathogens 65
20.1. Overview 65
20.2. Checklist of Dos and Don'ts 65

21. Dressing and Grooming Requirements 66
21.1. Overview 66
21.2. Checklist of Dos and Don'ts 66

22. Privacy, Technology and Transfer of Personal Data 66
22.1. Privacy Rights of Employees 66
22.2. Checklist of Dos and Don'ts 67

23. Workplace Investigations for Complaints of Discrimination, Harassment, Fraud, Theft and Whistle-Blowing 68
23.1. Overview 68
23.2. Checklist of Dos and Don'ts 69

24. Affirmative Action/Non-discrimination Requirements 69
24.1. Overview 69
24.2. Checklist of Dos and Don'ts 70

25. Resolution of Labour, Discrimination and Employment Disputes: Litigation, Arbitration, Mediation and Conciliation 70
25.1. Internal Dispute Resolution Process 70
25.2. Mediation and Conciliation 70
25.3. Arbitration 70
25.4. Litigation 71
25.5. Fines, Penalties and Damages 71
25.6. Checklist of Dos and Don'ts 72

26. Employer Recordkeeping, Data Protection and Employee Access to Personnel Files, and Records 72
26.1. Overview 72
26.2. Confidentiality Rules 75

27. Required Notices and Postings 75
27.1. Overview 75
27.2. Checklist of Dos and Don'ts 76

Ireland

AUTHORS

Duncan Inverarity

Duncan Inverarity is a Partner and Head of the Employment Law Group at A&L Goodbody Solicitors in Dublin, Ireland. He has considerable experience, having practised exclusively in the area of employment law and industrial relations in multiple jurisdictions.

He advises both public and private sector employers on both contentious and non-contentious matters. Duncan has developed close working relationships at the highest level with clients and provides strategic advice on restructuring, reorganization and general employment-related matters. He regularly appears in Employment Law fora, including the Workplace Relations Commission (WRC) and Labour Court. He also advises the public sector on administrative law matters and has regularly appeared in the High Court in high-profile judicial review proceedings.

Duncan speaks regularly on employment and industrial relations matters at conferences for organizations such as the Public Affairs Institute, Legal Island, the Law Society, and other professional bodies. He has co-authored *Employment Law in Ireland* and has written articles for specialist legal publications. He often provides comment on current employment issues in the national media. Duncan was involved in the establishment of the Law Society Employment Law diploma and now lectures on the course and to law students on the Law Society's Professional Practice Courses. He is also a member of the European Employment Lawyers Association and the Employment Lawyers Association of Ireland.

Tríona Sugrue

Tríona Sugrue is a Knowledge Lawyer in the Employment Practice Group at A&L Goodbody Solicitors in Dublin, Ireland. She has extensive experience in advising on all aspects of the employment relationship, contentious and non-contentious, including advising on complex workplace issues and representing clients in disputes before all employment-related fora.

Tríona's experience includes advising employers on a diverse range of matters relating to their workforces, including drafting bespoke employment contracts, agreements and HR policies and procedures, management of disciplinary issues, the handling of employee complaints, internal reorganizations and rationalizations, terminations, transfers of undertakings, atypical working arrangements and industrial relations issues.

Tríona is a regular speaker on a variety of employment law topics, both on behalf of A&L Goodbody and for the Law Society of Ireland, including lecturing on the Law Society Employment Law diploma and to trainee solicitors on the Professional Practice Course. Tríona is a committee member of the Dublin Solicitors Bar Association Employment Law Committee and the Employment Lawyers Association of Ireland.

ADDRESS

A&L Goodbody Solicitors
IFSC
North Wall Quay
Dublin 1
Tel.: +353 1 649 2000
Fax: +353 1649 2649
E-mail: dinverarity@algoodbody.com
Web: www.algoodbody.com

Legal Compliance in Ireland

1. LEGAL FRAMEWORK: EMPLOYMENT LAWS

Irish employment law operates in a highly regulated environment and is derived from a number of sources. Much of our legislation over the last number of years, particularly in the equality sphere, has been heavily influenced by our European obligations. The law of torts may also impose obligations on the employment relationship. The most obvious example of this is the duty of care employers owe employees for their safety while at work. Another factor which has also dictated the need for change has been the continuously evolving labour market and both employers' and employees' demands for flexibility in the workplace. This has resulted in the emergence of 'atypical' workers and various working patterns in the form of agency workers, part-time workers, and fixed-term workers. It has also contributed to the emergence of the 'gig economy'. This 'gig economy' is a way of working based on people doing temporary jobs or separate pieces of work if and when they decide.

The following are the principal sources of Irish employment law:

(1) *Common law*. This is law which has been developed by the courts or similar tribunals through judgments.
(2) *Statute law*. This is written law which is set down by the legislature in the form of Acts (the Oireachtas in Ireland is responsible for promulgating legislation).
(3) *Secondary legislation (Statutory Instruments)*. Such as regulations or orders made under Acts.
(4) *Bunreacht na hÉireann (the Irish Constitution)*. There are a number of constitutional provisions which are of direct relevance to the employment relationship such as Article 40.1 which states that all citizens are to be treated equally before the law.

(5) *Codes of Practice.* While these do not have binding legal effect, they may be taken into account by a court or a tribunal in reaching a decision.
(6) *EU Regulations and Directives.* Regulations have direct application in Ireland, and Directives are implemented into Irish law by way of primary legislation.
(7) *International Conventions.* An example of this is the European Convention on Human Rights, implemented in Ireland, by way of the European Convention on Human Rights Act 2003. This imposes an array of rights and freedoms on contracting parties. The primary ones of concern from an employment law perspective are the rights to privacy, fair procedures and freedom of association.
(8) As set out above, many of the employment statutes since the 1980s have resulted from Ireland's membership of the European Union (EU). These have taken the form principally of Directives but also have evolved in the form of decisions of the Court of Justice of the European Union (CJEU). It is from the Treaty of Rome that many directly applicable employment obligations arise such as the right to equal pay and so forth.

The judiciary is the branch of the Irish legal system which is responsible for compliance with the above sources of Irish law.

For the majority of employment law disputes, the Workplace Relations Commission (WRC) is the single point of entry for complaints, with the Labour Court being the sole appellate body. Decisions of the Labour Court may be appealed to the High Court on a point of law only (rather than re-hearing the entire case). Depending on the nature of the claim, employees may also have recourse to the Civil Courts directly.

2. CONTRACTS OF EMPLOYMENT

2.1. Overview

There is no universal definition of what constitutes an 'employment contract' or 'an employee'. Employment legislation commonly defines 'an employee' as a person engaged under a contract of employment and a 'contract of employment' as a contract of service or apprenticeship or a contract with an employment agency to personally provide work to a third party.[1] The contract of employment can be written or oral, express or

1. Terms of Employment (Information) Acts 1994–2014; Maternity Protection Acts 1994 and 2004; Adoptive Leave Acts 1995 and 2005; Carer's Leave Act 2001; Organisation of Working Time Act 1997; Parental Leave Acts 1998 and 2006; Protection of Young Persons (Employment) Act 1996; Payment of Wages Act 1991; National Minimum Wage Act 2000 and 2015; Protection of

implied. Similar to a standard contract, an employment contract comprises a number of core elements:

- Offer
- Acceptance
- Intention to create legal relations
- Consideration.

2.2. Written Employment Contracts

The Employment (Miscellaneous Provisions) Act 2018 requires employers to provide a new hire with a written statement notifying the employee of five core terms of employment within five days (as distinct from business days) from the commencement of employment (the *Written Statement*). These core terms are:

- names of employer and employee;
- address of employer;
- expected duration of temporary employment or the end date of a fixed-term contract;
- the method of calculating pay and pay reference period for the purposes of the National Minimum Wage Act 2000; and
- the number of hours which the employer 'reasonably expects' the employee to work: (i) per normal working day; and (ii) per normal working week.

This new requirement to provide Written Statement supplements existing notification requirements under the Terms of Employment (Information) Acts 1994–2014.

The Terms of Employment (Information) Acts 1994–2014 impose certain minimum obligations, namely that employers must furnish employees with certain terms and conditions of the employment relationship. In addition to the Written Statement, the employer must, within two months of the commencement of employment, give the employee a written statement of the terms and conditions of employment. This statement must include the following information:

(i) the names of employer and employee;
(ii) the address (or principal place of business) of the employer;
(iii) the place of work;

Employees (Part-Time) Work Act 2001; Redundancy Payment Acts 1967–2014; Employment Equality Acts 1998–2015; EC (Protection of Employees on Transfer of Undertakings) Regulations 2003.

(iv) the title of the job or nature of the work for which the employee is employed;
(v) the date of commencement of employment;
(vi) the duration of any temporary or fixed-term contract;
(vii) the rate or method of calculation of remuneration and pay reference period for the purposes of the National Minimum Wage Act 2000;
(viii) a reference to any registered employment agreement (REA) or employment regulation order (ERO) which applies to the employee and confirmation of where the employee may obtain such order;
(ix) whether remuneration is payable weekly, monthly or otherwise;
(x) any terms or conditions as to hours of work, including overtime;
(xi) any terms or conditions relating to paid leave (other than sick leave);
(xii) any terms or conditions relating to:
- incapacity for work due to sickness or injury;
- paid sick leave; and
- pensions and pension schemes.
(xiii) the period of notice which the employee must give or receive to terminate the employment;
(xiv) details of any collective agreements affecting the terms and conditions of employment.

In providing such a statement, it can be done by either letter of appointment or in the form of a more detailed contract. In reality, most employers incorporate their statutory obligations under this legislation into the contract of employment. Changes to any terms and conditions required by the Act must be notified to the employee within one month of taking effect. In addition, employers must, within twenty-eight days of the commencement of employment, give new staff a written summary of the procedures that would be used should it become necessary to carry out a dismissal under the Unfair Dismissal Acts 1977–2015. The document may include a provision for an initial probationary period. It would be usual to have a probationary term of six months, and in certain cases the employer may find it necessary to extend, in writing, that period. Employers should be aware, however, that on reaching twelve months' service, the employee in question will be eligible to bring a claim under the Unfair Dismissals legislation, regardless of whether they are on probation.

Any contract concluded in writing must also be compliant with Irish statutory law in relation to certain terms (e.g., minimum wage, notice periods – minimum notice periods are prescribed by law; however, an employer may at its discretion implement longer notice periods, and it would be usual for employers to give longer notice periods, particularly to those in more senior positions of employment).

2.3. Oral Contracts

There is nothing to prevent an employment contract from being oral in nature. However, the Terms of Employment (Information) Acts 1994–2014 require an employer to supply certain mandatory information detailing the nature of the relationship within two months from the commencement of the employment (*see* section 2.2 above).

2.4. Employee Handbooks

There is no legal requirement for an employer to have an employee handbook in place. However, as a matter of good human resource practice it is usually prudent to have one. The employee handbook contains information about company policy and procedure and is a useful way for a company to set out key information about the business, its ethos, and culture. Where an employer has an employee handbook in place it is important that it is kept up-to-date and reviewed regularly. Employers should also ensure that employees are aware of its contents and that its contents are communicated in an appropriate medium (e.g., via company intranet) to employees.

Ideally, the policies set out within the handbook should not form part of an employee's terms and conditions of employment to facilitate the employer when seeking to revise the content of those policies. The handbook should expressly state that it does not form part of an employee's terms and conditions of employment and should state that if there is any conflict between an employee's contract and the handbook, the employee's contract should take precedence.

2.5. Job Descriptions

Generally, job descriptions are drafted widely to allow the employer a degree of flexibility in effecting minor changes to an employee's role. However, caution should be taken in relation to this approach because, if redundancies were subsequently implemented, employees could argue that their job function obliged them to carry out different duties from those duties which had become redundant.

2.6. Offer Letters

Once a decision has been made to offer employment, the candidate should be furnished with a letter setting out the terms upon which employment is being offered.

2.7. Checklist of Dos and Don'ts

- Ensure core terms in accordance with the Employment (Miscellaneous Provisions) Act 2018 are furnished in writing within five days of commencing employment.
- Ensure letter/contract complying with the Terms of Employment (Information) Acts 1994–2014 is furnished within two months of commencing employment.
- Ensure employee handbook is kept up-to-date, reviewed regularly and that it is a 'live' document.
- Employers should ensure handbook contents are communicated regularly to all employees.

3. RECRUITING, INTERVIEWING, SCREENING AND HIRING EMPLOYEES

3.1. Overview

In theory, employers can choose who they wish to recruit. However, the development of equality laws, intertwined with the huge amount of information available on social media, has led to the recruitment process becoming a more cautious and considered exercise for employers.

3.2. Recruiting

An employer's ability to recruit is constrained by provisions of the equality legislation. In advertising and in ultimately determining who to appoint, an employer must not discriminate on any of the nine grounds set out under the Employment Equality Acts 1998–2015. Those grounds are:

(1) Gender.
(2) Civil Status.
(3) Family Status.
(4) Sexual Orientation.
(5) Religion.

(6) Age.
(7) Disability.
(8) Race/colour/nationality/ethnic or national origins.
(9) Membership of the Traveller Community.

3.3. Employment Applications

The Employment Equality Acts prohibit discrimination not only in the employment sphere but in the context of 'access to employment' – i.e., recruitment. Job advertisements should not contain discriminatory wording. An advertisement seeking a 'young and dynamic professional' previously was held to have breached the Employment Equality Acts.

The exception to this rule is where there is a determining occupational requirement that the position be filled by a person with specific characteristics (e.g., *male versus female* or vice versa). The Acts permit positive action in these circumstances, although an employer must be able to prove that the requirement is genuine. In addition, the Acts allow for positive action measures to prevent or compensate for disadvantages linked to any of the other discriminatory grounds, including protecting the health and safety at work of persons with a disability, or to create or maintain facilities for safeguarding or promoting the integration of disabled employees into the working environment.

3.4. Pre-employment Inquiries

Social media websites, such as Facebook and Twitter, have vastly increased the amount of easily accessible information available about potential employees. Employers can obtain a huge amount of information about a potential recruit that would not be available on their CV such as marital status, whether they have dependants, their race. Relying on information obtained in this way to influence a hiring decision may raise issues relating to data protection and employment equality matters.

Any pre-employment background checks will need to be conducted in accordance with the recent EU General Data Protection Regulation (GDPR) and the Data Protection Act 2018.

Any verification process carried out by an employer should be transparent. Applicants should be told what information may be verified and how it may be verified.

3.5. Pre-employment Tests and Examinations

Prior to offering employment to a candidate, employers may wish to consider the appropriateness of seeking medical certification of a candidate's fitness to perform the role. Care should be taken, from a data protection and employment equality perspective, when ascertaining whether such a pre-employment medical is required. Where the employee may be suffering from a disability, consideration of what measures of reasonable accommodation could be put in place to assist the employee in carrying out the requisite role will be required. An employer is required to regard a person with a disability as fully competent to undertake and be fully capable of undertaking any duties if, by taking 'appropriate measures', that person would be fully competent and fully capable of undertaking those duties. There are, however, some exceptions to this, namely where such appropriate measures would impose a disproportionate burden on the employer.

In determining whether the measures would impose such a burden, account should be taken of: (i) the financial and other costs entailed; (ii) the scale and financial resources of the employer's business; and (iii) the possibility of obtaining public funding or other assistance.

3.6. Background, Reference, and Credit Checks

Employers should exercise caution when conducting background checks on employees, as it is an offence to compel a potential employee to make an access request, such as to the Irish police, and to reveal the response.

All personal or previous employment references should be checked prior to offering employment. A duty of care is owed to a future prospective employer as well as the employee by someone giving a reference. There is no guarantee that references will remain confidential as they can often be sought by the subject through a data subject access request (DSAR). This has made many (particularly large) employers reluctant to give any written reference beyond a standard 'Statement of Employment' type reference, whether the employee was good, bad or indifferent. These simply state the period of employment and position held. Referees should even be careful with 'off the record' requests for their views.

Criminal background checks can only be carried out in Ireland by the Garda (Irish police) National Vetting Bureau. The National Vetting Bureau (Children and Vulnerable Persons) Act 2012 is the main legislation which governs Garda vetting in Ireland. The legislation applies to those whose work involves having access to, or contact with, children or vulnerable persons.

Under the Data Protection Act 2018 it is an offence for an employer to force an employee (or potential employee) to make a data access request to the Gardai and to reveal the response. If data in relation to an 'employee's criminal convictions is processed by an employer, it must be done in compliance with the GDPR and the Data Protection Act 2018. Such processing is only permissible where one of the six lawful bases for processing under Article 6 GDPR and one of the five legal bases for processing criminal data under section 55 of the Data Protection Act 2018 have been identified. Consent is generally an unreliable legal basis in an employment context due to the imbalance of power between the employer and the employee and the fact that a data subject can revoke their consent at any time.

Criminal background checks on prospective employees are rarely carried out in Ireland, and there is no register of criminal convictions which an employer can access. As the law currently stands, an employer can ask a prospective employee to self-declare any previous criminal convictions, subject to the Spent Convictions Act (as detailed below). Under the Data Protection Act 2018, it remains possible to process such data where certain conditions are met, including that the processing is *necessary and proportionate for the performance of a contract* to which the data subject is a party. As above, only employers in regulated sectors dealing with children or vulnerable adults can request the police to carry out criminal background checks.

The GDPR and Ireland's implementing legislation (the Data Protection Act 2018) have had a significant impact on the responsibilities of employers with regard to the processing of personal data, which, for the purpose of GDPR, is any data relating to an identified or identifiable natural person.

The GDPR must be observed in respect of information sought – including backgrounds, references and credit checks – and the subsequent retention periods of such information.

3.7. The Criminal Justice (Spent Convictions and Certain Disclosures) Act 2016

The Criminal Justice (Spent Convictions and Certain Disclosures) Act 2016 provides that an individual does not have to disclose certain criminal convictions which date back seven years or more to a future or current employer. The Act ensures that only certain convictions arising from minor offences can become 'spent'. The following offences will never become 'spent': a conviction for a sexual offence, an offence tried in the Central Criminal Court, and an offence resulting in a prison sentence of greater than twelve months. This Act also impacts how employers screen future employees.

3.8. Interviewing

In any interview, interviewers should avoid potentially discriminatory topics and concentrate on objective criteria such as skill sets, track record, experience and qualifications. An employer should keep detailed notes of the interview process, and these notes should record objective, balanced and salient comments. If an employer can produce documents showing objective fair selection criteria then if a discriminatory question is asked an employer may be able to show that it had no overall effect on the ultimate decision-making process. As the burden of proof rests with the employer, they will have a much more difficult case to defend if it has no paper trail to support its position.

3.9. Hiring Procedures

Employers must avoid referring to or basing a hiring decision on any discriminatory characteristics of the candidate. Employers also need to carefully consider the scope of requests for personal information from applicants and ensure such requests are in line with the Data Protection Act 2018. Any particularly sensitive information that is requested (such as criminal convictions or information regarding medical history) must be directly relevant to the recruitment decision or the particular job. The prohibition on enforced data access requests means that it is an offence to attempt to require an employee or prospective employee to make an access request or reveal the results of such request.

3.10. Fines and Penalties

The Employment Equality Acts prohibit discrimination on any of the nine grounds in relation to access to employment. An award of up to EUR 13,000 may be made if a claimant applicant succeeds in a claim under this head.

3.11. Checklist of Dos and Don'ts

- Be careful in the wording of any job advertisement.
- Avoid any potentially discriminatory questions at the interview stage.

- Keep detailed notes of what is said during the interview process.
- Employers should review their recruitment procedures to ensure that their recruitment processes, employment application and screening process do not entail enforced data access requests.

4. MANAGING PERFORMANCE/CONDUCT

4.1. Overview

There is no prescribed statutory process under Irish law for dealing with underperforming employees. Termination of employment for performance-related reasons is a permitted reason for dismissal although it is not easy to establish. It will usually require the employer to have given the employee a number of opportunities to improve and have engaged in the following:

- a formal Performance Improvement Process (PIP); and
- a disciplinary process.

As a result, performance-related dismissals in Ireland can be slow and time-consuming.

4.2. Coaching and Counselling

If an employee is not performing to a level, an employer is entitled to reasonably expect, then it may be necessary for a PIP to be initiated with the employee. A PIP is a HR tool designed to measure and encourage performance. Under Irish law the objective of the PIP is to afford the employee the chance to improve before any disciplinary process might be considered.

4.3. Written Evaluations

As part of the PIP and as part of general employee assessments an employer should conduct written evaluations of all employees.

4.4. Warnings and Suspensions

If following the PIP process an employee's performance has not sufficiently improved, the employer may commence the first step in the disciplinary process, i.e., an oral warning. A brief note of the oral warning should be issued. The next stage is a written warning. The employee should have a right of appeal against all sanctions. If there is still no sufficient improvement the employee can be issued with a final written warning again with a right of appeal. This warning should make clear that if there is no improvement the employment may be terminated. Prior to issuing any disciplinary sanctions, it is imperative the employee is given an opportunity to state their case and be accompanied by a colleague or trade union representative, if they choose.

4.5. Checklist of Dos and Don'ts

- Ensure the employee knows why the PIP process is being initiated.
- Ensure the employee is afforded sufficient time to make appropriate improvements (this may include access to additional training, additional support such as the allocation of a buddy or mentoring system).

5. TERMINATION OF EMPLOYEES FOR PERFORMANCE OR DISCIPLINARY REASONS

5.1. Overview

If, following the above procedure, an employee's performance does not sufficiently improve, the employment may be terminated on giving appropriate notice, by giving either the employee's statutory or contractual notice entitlement, whichever is longer. There is a statutory presumption that a dismissal under Irish law is unfair. In certain limited circumstances, a dismissal can be deemed to be fair where it is for one of the following reasons:

- capability (relating to the employee's capability to perform the role);
- competence (relating to the employee's ability and skill to perform the role);
- conduct (relating to the employee's poor conduct in connection with their employment);
- redundancy;
- that the employer or employee was prohibited by statute from continuing to employ the individual in their job;
- or if the dismissal did not result wholly or mainly from one or more of the above matters there must have been some other substantial ground justifying the dismissal.

If lawful grounds exist for a dismissal, then the employer must follow certain fair procedures before giving notice of termination. The employer must be able to demonstrate that it has acted reasonably in coming to the decision to dismiss and that the dismissal is within a range of reasonable responses open to the employer in the circumstances.

5.2. Separation/Severance Pay

In some performance-related dismissals employers do not wish to invest the time in the improvement process when they do not really believe that the performance will improve. This is particularly so with more senior employees. In such cases, severance agreements with a termination payment to the affected employee may ultimately be agreed, but this has to be very carefully approached, and independent legal advice should be sought in such situations.

5.3. Fines and Penalties

An employee may allege that they were unfairly dismissed and bring an unfair dismissal claim. If successful, the Workplace Relation Commission (WRC) could award up to two years' gross remuneration (salary, bonus and benefits), reinstatement or re-engagement. Claimants have a duty to mitigate their loss.

5.4. Checklist of Dos and Don'ts

- Encourage and conduct regular appraisals of staff.
- Allow sufficient time for an employee who is subject to a PIP to improve before taking any action in relation to termination.
- If a decision to dismiss is ultimately reached, ensure fair procedures are applied to the termination process.

6. LAYOFFS, REDUCTIONS IN FORCE AND/OR REDUNDANCIES AS A RESULT OF JOB ELIMINATIONS OR OTHER RESTRUCTURING

6.1. Overview

Redundancy is broadly defined under Irish law and can occur in a number of situations, including the following:

- an employer ceases to carry on its business in part or entirely; or
- work requirements have diminished; or
- work is to be done in a different manner for which the affected employee is not qualified; or
- work is to be done by a different person who already performs other work for which the affected employee is not qualified; or
- work is to be done at a different location.

6.2. Reductions in Force/Layoffs/Job Eliminations

The key feature of a genuine redundancy situation is that it is the position rather than the person who becomes redundant. If the person is to be replaced, this would indicate that it is probably not a valid redundancy as there is an element of subjectivity in the decision to dismiss. Termination of employment for performance or other reasons related to the individual is unlikely to be viewed a valid redundancy.

There is no genuine redundancy situation:

- if the employee's contract is renewed; or
- if the employee is re-engaged under a new contract by the same employer and the new arrangement is to take effect immediately; or
- if the renewal or re-engagement follows an offer in writing made by the employer before the ending of the current contract and the new contract takes effect immediately or no later than four weeks from the end of the previous contract.

Specific statutory redundancy rights exist for employees. These rights include:

- Consultation with the employee before the employer makes a decision. This is a recommended best practice in individual redundancy situations. It is particularly advisable where there is selection between a number of employees. Consultation is a statutory obligation in 'collective redundancies'.
- Notice of termination of employment.

- Redundancy lump sum payment (if applicable).
- Paid time off to look for alternative employment or arrange for training.

A valid redundancy is a fair dismissal, but the burden of proof is on the employer to show:

- the redundancy was genuine;
- objective criteria were applied in selecting employees for redundancy;
- reasonable alternatives to redundancy were considered (such as redeployment within the business).

Accordingly, it is important for the employer to consult appropriately with affected employees before making decisions on redundancy. This is particularly so where a selection exercise is necessary.

Factors to be considered in selecting employees for redundancy can include the following:

- Skills.
- Qualifications.
- Experience.
- Adaptability to different work.

Many employers when approaching redundancy selection use a detailed assessment system awarding marks under each relevant category to the various employees who are being considered and those with the lowest marks are selected for redundancy. This assists in showing that an employer applied an objective methodology in assessing which individuals should be made redundant. The employee in question should ideally have an input into this process. Previous annual reviews or other assessments may prove objective sources of information in 'scoring' employees against the criteria.

Length of service may also be a valid factor, especially where, having applied other criteria, employees have equal scores.

Ideally disciplinary records should generally not be taken into account. Furthermore, discriminatory grounds such as age, civil status, family status, or disability are automatically unfair grounds. Employers have to be particularly careful regarding individual employees who are pregnant, or on maternity leave, or absent due to illness as additional issues can arise in those cases. A note should be kept of any meetings and any internal communications in order to demonstrate the fairness of the process followed.

Employers are not legally obliged to pay anything on top of the statutory entitlements. However, voluntary 'top-up' or 'ex gratia' payments are reasonably commonplace in Ireland. The amount of any such payment is a matter for the employer to determine, but that decision may be influenced by such issues as custom and practice in the business or its industry sector. It is usual for an employer to require that a severance agreement is entered into where an ex gratia payment is made.

6.3. Collective Redundancies

Irish law imposes a number of information and consultation obligations on an employer where it is effecting a 'collective redundancy'. A 'collective redundancy' is one that involves making a specified number of employees redundant within a thirty consecutive day period. The thresholds are set out below:

Total Workforce	*Threshold Number of Redundancies*
20–49	5 or more
50–99	10 or more
100–299	10% or more of the workforce
300 or more	30 or more

Where the employer conducts collective bargaining with a trade union that represents the affected employees, it consults with the trade union. If, however, there is no such union relationship, the employer must put in place an arrangement enabling the affected employees to select their representatives.

An employer must provide the following information to the representatives:

- the reasons for the proposed redundancies;
- the number and descriptions or categories of employees whom it is proposed to make redundant;
- the number and descriptions or categories of employees normally employed;
- the period during which it is proposed to effect the redundancies;
- the proposed selection criteria;
- the method proposed for calculating redundancy payments.

Consultation must be 'initiated at the earliest opportunity', and in any event at least thirty days before the first notice of dismissal is given. Consultation must be on the proposed collective redundancies, with a view to reaching an agreement. The consultations must include discussion on the possibility of avoiding the proposed redundancies, reducing the numbers of employees affected, and the basis on which it will be decided which particular employees will be made redundant. In addition, 'at the earliest opportunity' and in any event at least thirty days before the first dismissal takes effect, the employer must give specific notice to the relevant minister (and copy that to the employee representatives). This information largely mirrors that listed above, but with some additional requirements. The Minister has the power to make further enquiries and seek consultation with the employer about the situation and to carry out investigations if necessary but does not usually avail of that power.

6.4. Fines and Penalties

All eligible employees are entitled to a lump sum based on their pay. They are entitled to two weeks' pay per year of service plus one further week's pay. The amount of statutory redundancy is subject to a maximum earnings limit of EUR 600 per week. Section 6(4)(c) of the Unfair Dismissals Acts says that a dismissal is fair if it results wholly or mainly from the redundancy of an employee. The employer, however, bears the burden of proof in establishing the legitimacy of any redundancy dismissal. In addition to this, the employer must also bear the burden of establishing that the employee was fairly selected for redundancy and that fair procedures were followed in carrying out any redundancies. If an employee succeeds in claiming that it was not a fair dismissal on the redundancy grounds then the usual remedies from the WRC would apply, up to two years' gross remuneration, re-engagement or reinstatement.

In a collective redundancy situation, failure to initiate consultation with the employees' representatives, or to notify the Minister, is an offence and an employer is liable on summary conviction to a fine not exceeding EUR 5,000. An employee, trade union, staff association or excepted body may present a complaint to the WRC arising out of a failure to inform and consult concerning collective redundancies. The WRC can direct the employer to pay compensation to an employee as is just and equitable but not exceeding four weeks' remuneration in respect of the employee's employment. An employer who implements a collective redundancy before the expiry of the thirty-day notice period in relation to notification to the Minister is guilty of an offence and liable on conviction to a fine not exceeding EUR 250,000.

6.5. Checklist of Dos and Don'ts

– Once a genuine redundancy situation is identified, an employer has a duty to ensure that the selection process is fair and also has a duty to act reasonably. The duty to act reasonably involves a number of elements, including the following: they must consult with and engage with the affected employee(s), consider alternatives, and in some cases offer a right of appeal from the redundancy decision itself.

- Once an employee meets the necessary qualifying criteria (i.e., two years' service) ensure they are afforded appropriate notice, statutory redundancy pay, paid time to look for alternative employment or arrange for training and compensation for any other accrued rights, including untaken annual leave, etc.
- In a collective redundancy situation, employers should ensure that the time limits regarding information and consultation obligations to employees and the Minister are complied with.

7. LABOUR AND EMPLOYMENT LAW RAMIFICATIONS UPON ACQUISITION OR SALE OF A BUSINESS

7.1. Overview

The main impact of the sale or acquisition of a business from an employment law perspective concerns what happens to the employees. The law relating to transfers of undertakings comes from European law and is designed to safeguard employees' rights when businesses (or parts of them) are taken over. The various Directives have been transposed into Irish law by way of the European Communities (Protection of Employees on Transfer of Undertakings) Regulations 2003 as amended (the Regulations).

The Regulations apply to any legal transfer of any undertaking, business, or part of an undertaking or business from one employer to another. A transfer can be by way of a lease or licence, franchise, or other arrangement. There does not necessarily have to be a change of ownership. However it is essential to establish if there has been a change of employer: this is a fundamental prerequisite to the application of the Regulations. A change of employer may occur in a contracting out or similar situation. Similarly, a change of employer can, and generally does occur, within the context of an intra-group transfer. As a general rule, a share purchase alone does not attract the Regulations as it does not involve a change of employer.

In determining whether or not there has been a change of employer the court will not be deterred by devices such as service companies or by complicated group structures which conceal the true relationship such as a situation where, in a company belonging to a group, employees are employed by one company but working on a permanent basis for another. In those circumstances, if the company for whom the employee works on a permanent basis is transferred, that employee also transfers.

The Regulations can apply to the transfer of subsidiary or ancillary activities, such as outsourcing, cleaning, or catering services, provided the transferring business is an 'economic entity'. This can even be the case where only one employee transfers. The term 'undertaking' encompasses any entity engaged in economic activity regardless of the legal status of that entity and regardless as to whether the entity is profit or non-profit making. This definition brings the following within the Regulations: charities, local authorities, health boards, state and semi-state bodies, education establishments, medical establishments and foundations, trade associations, and trade unions. The Regulations apply to the transfer of an economic entity that retains its identity. Economic entity is defined as an organized grouping of resources that has the objective of pursuing an economic activity, whether or not that activity is for profit or whether it is central or ancillary to another economic or administrative entity. The business in question must retain its identity after the transfer and must be classifiable as a stable economic entity with an ongoing life rather than a short-term contractual enterprise.

7.2. Acquisition of a Business

In most cases when you acquire a business you are required to take on the workforce. A detailed audit of the target business should be conducted at the earliest opportunity and a list compiled of all transferring employees with as much consideration as possible given to each of the employees concerned and their future in the business.

The employees' rights and obligations arising from the contract of employment transfer to the transferee. The transferee is prevented from making changes to the employees' terms and conditions as a result of the transfer.

The transfer of an undertaking, business or part of a business does not in itself constitute grounds for dismissal. However, nothing in the Regulations prohibits a dismissal if the new employer can justify such dismissal for economic, technical or organizational (ETO) reasons. Whether there are such ETO reasons for the dismissal will depend on the facts of each case. Accordingly, it is difficult for employers to justify any changes in advance of a sale in order to make the business more attractive.

The new employer is obliged to comply with any collective agreement in force at the time of the transfer. The transfer of an undertaking does not break an employee's continuity of service and the employee's continuity is therefore preserved. The liability of the old employer for personal injury transfers to the new employer on a transfer of undertakings.

The Regulations do not apply to employees' rights to old-age, invalidity or survivors benefits under supplementary or inter-company pension schemes falling outside the Social Welfare Acts. However, the Regulations do impose an obligation on a transferee to ensure that the interests of employees, and of persons no longer employed in the transferor's business, are protected in respect of rights conferring on them immediate or prospective entitlement to old-age benefits, including survivors' benefits.

Where the transfer is likely to impact the new 'employer's current workforce it has an obligation to undertake the same information and consultation process vis-à-vis those employees (details of which are set out below) and within the same time limits.

7.3. Acquisition Checklist

- Conduct audit of the business to identify transferring lists of employees, nature of liabilities, etc.
- Ensure obligations regarding information and consultation are complied with within the appropriate time periods prescribed.

7.4. Sale of a Business

The transfer of the employee from transferor to transferee is automatic, irrespective of the wishes of either party. This is subject only to the right of the employee to object to a transfer of their employment relationship. EU case law says that employees are entitled to object to the transfer of their employment contract but the legal effect of this objection is a matter for each Member State to determine. In the event that an employee objects to the transfer without cause there is no entitlement to a redundancy payment from either the transferor or the transferee in such circumstances.

The Regulations create specific information and consultation obligations in the context of the transfers of businesses. Employees attaching to a business or part of a business that is transferring from one employer to another employer have the protection of the Regulations, and transfer with their accrued service and current terms and conditions to the new employer. However, before the transfer can take place, particular information and consultation obligations arise.

The obligation is to inform employee representatives. These are defined as 'a trade union, staff association or excepted body with which it has been the practice of the employees' employer to conduct collective bargaining negotiations'. However, there are of course occasions where employers do not have collective bargaining practices, and in those cases the Regulations provide that the representatives are to be 'a person or persons chosen by such employees' (under an arrangement put in place by the employer) from among their number to represent them in negotiations with the employer. The information that must be given to the representatives is as follows:

(i) the date or proposed date of the transfer;
(ii) the reasons for the transfer;
(iii) the legal implications of the transfer for the employees and a summary of any relevant economic and social implications of the transfer for them;
(iv) any measures envisaged in relation to the employees; and
(v) certain details regarding any agency workers engaged in the business.

This information must be given to the representatives 'where reasonably practicable, not later than thirty days before the transfer is carried out, and in any event, in good time before the transfer is carried out'.

Consultation only arises where it is anticipated that there will be any 'measures' in relation to the employees. Again, consultation in this context must take place 'where reasonably practicable, not later than thirty days before the transfer is carried out and, in any event, in good time before the transfer is carried out, in relation to any such measures with a view to reaching an agreement'. The Regulations do not define what is meant by 'measures', but one has to assume that this refers to material changes that might arise for the employees.

It should also be noted that the consultation is stated to be 'with a view to reaching an agreement'. The Regulations do not spell out what might happen if an agreement is not reached. It is doubtful, however, whether a transfer could be permanently blocked for a failure to reach an agreement. It is possible, however, that in certain cases an injunction might be sought which could have the effect of delaying a transfer taking place.

If the employer has made efforts to enable the employees select a representative or representatives from among their number, but none have been selected, then each of the employees is entitled to be informed in writing within the timescales referred to above of the information as set out above. Good practice would dictate that in any case, even those where there are representatives, it would be advisable for employers to ensure that the information that is being given to representatives is at the same time relayed to each employee in order to ensure that the employees receive the information in exactly the way the employer wants it to be received, rather than through the filter of a third-party representative.

Where there has been a failure to consult, the WRC to whom a complaint has been made by the employee or by their trade union/staff association can make an award of compensation to the employee of an amount not exceeding four weeks' remuneration. While this might not appear to be a large amount of compensation, it might be very considerable if there is a particularly large workforce where the employer has failed to comply with its information and consultation obligations.

7.5. Sale Checklist

- Ensure time limits regarding obligations to inform and consult with the workforce are adhered to.
- If the new or old employer involved in a transfer envisages measures in relation to the employees, they must consult representatives of the employees where reasonably practicable no later than thirty days before the transfer occurs and in any event in good time with a view to seeking agreement.
- Negotiate warranties and indemnities in respect of risk issues.

8. USE OF ALTERNATIVE WORKFORCES: INDEPENDENT CONTRACTORS, CONTRACT EMPLOYEES AND TEMPORARY OR LEASED WORKERS

8.1. Overview

The dynamics of the Irish labour market have changed considerably over the past number of years. As a result both employers' and employees' demands for flexibility in their status have led to the growth of 'atypical' workers and working patterns in the form of agency workers, independent contractors, part-time workers and fixed-term workers.

8.2. Independent Contractors

It can be difficult to determine if someone is an employee or an independent contractor. Given that a person must establish 'employee' status in order to avail of the many protections employment law affords, determining such status is crucial. An employee is generally defined as someone who works under a 'contract of employment'. However there is no universal definition in Irish legislation of what constitutes an employment contract. Various pieces of legislation have defined it as someone working under a 'contract of service or apprenticeship or a contract with an employment agency to personally provide work to a third party'.[2] In order to assist in determining the status of an employee a number of tests have been developed by the

2. Terms of Employment (Information) Acts 1994–2014; Maternity Protection Acts 1994 and 2004; Adoptive Leave Acts 1995 and 2005; Carer's Leave Act 2001; Organisation of Working Time Act 1997; Parental Leave Acts 1998 and 2006; Protection of Young Persons (Employment) Act 1996; Payment of Wages Act 1991; National Minimum Wage Act 2000 and 2015; Protection of Employees (Part-Time) Work Act 2001; Redundancy Payment Acts 1967–2014; Employment Equality Acts 1998–2015; EC (Protection of Employees on Transfer of Undertakings) Regulations 2003.

courts. These tests are generally not conclusive of the issue, as each case tends to turn on its own factual circumstances.

The terms of any written agreement between the parties will undoubtedly assist in determining the employment relationship which is created. However, it is well established in Irish case law that the written intentions of the parties are only one part of the overall assessment as to the nature of the actual working relationship and the characterization almost wholly depends on an assessment of the substance of the relationship as it actually operates in practice. The High Court confirmed that there is no single test which will determine the latter conclusively.[3]

Some of the features which the Court will look at in order to decipher the exact nature of the relationship between the employer and employee are as follows:

(i) Has the worker agreed to perform work for the employer and has the employer agreed to provide work to that particular worker on an ongoing basis? This is referred to as the mutuality of obligation test.

(ii) Is the worker in business on their own account? This is the so-called enterprise test. This means if a worker is free to determine the manner in which the work is carried out (this includes the adding or taking away of staff) then this points to the position that it is a genuine contractor relationship and not an employee relationship.

(iii) Does the worker use their own equipment or the employer's equipment?

(iv) Does the worker perform the work from the employer's premises?

(v) Does the employer exercise day-to-day control over the employee and how the work is performed? For example, involvement in rostering, monitoring working hours, monitoring performance, all tend to infer that an employment relationship exists.

(vi) Another issue to be looked at is the way in which tax and Pay Related Social Insurance (PRSI) is payable to the Revenue. An employee will have tax and PRSI deducted from their income. A self-employed person is obliged to pay preliminary tax and file income returns whether or not they are asked for them.

The Revenue Commissioners have also published a useful guide designed to assist in determining whether someone is an employee or an independent contractor.[4]

3. *The Minister for Agriculture and Food v. Barry & Ors* [2008] IEHC 7 Jul. 2008.

4. https://www.revenue.ie/en/self-assessment-and-self-employment/documents/code-of-practice-on-employment-status.pdf.

8.3. Contract Workers/Fixed-Term Contract

Fixed-term contracts are frequently used in Ireland, but, with the implementation in 2003 of protective legislation, they are somewhat less attractive for employers. Such contracts can have great benefits for employers and can be very suitable for use in various situations including:

(i) Replacing employees on temporary leave such as maternity or parental leave or on career breaks.
(ii) Engaging employees for specific temporary projects or to fulfil specific orders for limited periods.
(iii) For temporary situations where the employer has a specific operational need for an employee for only a limited period and is unlikely to seek to extend such employment.

Fixed-term employees do not enjoy protection against unfair dismissal on the expiry of the fixed-term where their written contract contains a specific provision stating that the Unfair Dismissals Acts do not apply to a dismissal which occurs only as a result of the contract reaching its end date or completing its specified purpose and the contract is signed by both parties. It is important to note that the contract of employment of a fixed-term worker may be scrutinized by the WRC and deemed an open-ended contract in the guise of a fixed-term contract.

A fixed-term contract is determined by an objective condition such as arriving at a specific date, completing a specific task or the occurrence of a specific event. The definition does not include employees in initial vocational training relationships or apprenticeship schemes or employees with a contract of employment which has been concluded within the framework of a specific public or publicly supported training, integration, or vocational retraining programme.

A fixed-term employee may not, in respect of their conditions of employment, be treated in a less favourable manner (which may include the renewal of a fixed-term contract for a further fixed-term) than a comparable permanent employee unless that treatment can be justified on objective grounds. 'Conditions of employment' include remuneration, benefits and bonuses. Fixed-term employees who work less than 20% of the hours of a comparable permanent employee may be treated less favourably with regard to pension schemes or arrangements.

A fixed-term employee should be informed of any vacancies or training opportunities which may arise so that the fixed-term worker has the same opportunity as other employees to secure a permanent job.

An employee is a comparable permanent employee if he is:

(a) employed by the same or an associated employer, and one of (i), (ii) or (iii) below is satisfied; or
(b) specified in a collective agreement to be regarded as such; or
(c) employed in the same industry or sector of employment as the fixed-term employee and one of (i), (ii) or (iii) below is satisfied.

The conditions referred to at (a) and (c) above are that:

(i) both employees (i.e., the fixed-term employee and the comparable permanent employee) perform the same work or each is interchangeable with the other;
(ii) the work done by both employees is of the same or a similar nature, and any differences between the work or the conditions under which it is performed are of small importance or occur with insignificant irregularity; and
(iii) the work performed by the fixed-term employee is equal or greater in value to the work performed by the other employee, having regard to such matters as skill, physical or mental requirements, responsibility and working conditions.

A fixed-term employee must be informed in writing by their employer of the objective condition that will terminate the contract of employment. An employer must also confirm in writing the objective grounds justifying the renewal of a fixed-term contract as opposed to offering a contract of indefinite duration.

Where a fixed-term employee completes or has completed their third year of continuous employment with the employer, their contract may be renewed by that employer on only one occasion and any such renewal can only be for a fixed-term of no longer than one year. Where a fixed-term employee is employed on two or more continuous fixed-term contracts the aggregate duration of the contracts cannot exceed four years. Thereafter, the contract is considered to be permanent. This does not apply to the renewal of a contract for a fixed-term where there are objective grounds justifying such a renewal.

An objective ground has to be based on considerations other than the status of the employee. The less favourable treatment has to be for the purpose of achieving a legitimate objective of the employer, and the means chosen to achieve the objective have to be appropriate and necessary for that purpose.

To objectively justify less favourable treatment an employer needs to show that it is for a legitimate business reason, and that the measures he has taken are appropriate and necessary (not just desirable). This requires the employer to show that there were no alternative means having a less discriminatory effect by which the objective could have been achieved.

Part-Time Workers

Part-time employees (i.e., a person whose normal hours of work are less than the normal hours of work of a comparable employee) are entitled to be treated no less favourably than a comparable full-time colleague unless such less favourable treatment can be objectively justified.

A comparable employee is a full-time employee to whom a part-time employee compares himself who is:

(a) employed by the same employer or associated employers and one of the conditions referred to below is satisfied; or
(b) where (a) does not apply the permanent employee is specified in a collective agreement to be a type of employee who is to be regarded for the purposes of the Protection of Employees (Part-Time Work) Act 2001 as a comparable full-time employee; or
(c) where (a) and (b) do not apply the employee is employed in the same industry or sector of employment and who is doing either identical, similar work or work of equal value.

Conditions:

(a) both of the employees concerned perform the same work under the same or similar conditions or each is interchangeable with the other;
(b) the work performed is of the same or a similar nature and any differences are of small importance or are so irregular they are insignificant; and
(c) the work performed by the part-time employee is equal or greater in value to the work performed by the other employee concerned.

Part-time employees who work less than 20% of the hours of a comparable full-time employee may be treated less favourably with regard to pension schemes or arrangements.

A casual part-time worker may be employed on less favourable terms than a comparable full-time employee so long as there is an objective justification for so doing.[5] The Act envisages that the objective grounds in the case of a casual part-time employee may be less stringent than those for a non-casual part-time employee. This has been interpreted to mean that expense (which would not be a ground of objective business justification in the case of an ordinary part-time worker) might qualify as a ground in the case of a casual worker.

A worker is regarded as casual where the worker has been in continuous employment for less than thirteen weeks, and the period of service, and any previous period of service, could not reasonably be regarded as regular or seasonal employment.

5. Sections 11 and 12 Protection of Employees (Part-Time Work) Act 2001.

8.4. Leased Workers

The concept in Ireland is referred to as agency workers. An agency worker is generally deemed to be an employee of the agency which supplied the agency worker to the firm for whom they are carrying out the work. Workers engaged through agencies are covered in the same way as direct employees under a range of legislation including those that deal with payment of wages, unfair dismissal, maternity protection, adoptive leave, hours of work and equality.

However, it is important to note that for the purposes of unfair dismissal and health and safety legislation the employer of the agency workers will be deemed to be the firm they are working for rather than the employment agency. Under the Unfair Dismissals legislation, an agency worker (like any other employee) is generally not entitled to take an unfair dismissal claim until they have twelve months' service. In respect of social welfare payments, an agency worker is employed by the person who pays their wages.[6]

Agency workers are entitled to the same basic working terms and conditions of employment as if they were directly hired by the hirer. The Protection of Employees (Temporary Agency Work) Act 2012 provides that, all agency workers are entitled to the same basic pay as if they were employed by the hirer.

Pay means 'basic pay' and 'any pay in excess of basic pay' in respect of:

- shift work;
- piece work;
- overtime;
- unsocial hours worked; and
- hours worked on a Sunday.

It does not include:

- sick pay;
- payments under any pension scheme or arrangement; and
- payments under financial participation schemes.

Basic working and employment conditions are terms and conditions required to be included in a contract of employment by virtue of any legislation or collective agreement or any arrangement relating to:

- pay;
- working time;
- rest periods;
- rest breaks during the working day;

6. Social Welfare (Miscellaneous Provisions) Act 2003.

- night work;
- overtime;
- annual leave;
- public holidays.

In addition to equal treatment in relation to basic working and employment conditions, the hirer of the agency worker is obliged under section 14 of the 2012 Act to treat an agency worker no less favourably than an employee of the hirer, (unless the difference in treatment can be objectively justified), in relation to access to collective facilities and amenities at a place of work including:

- canteen or other similar facilities;
- childcare facilities;
- transport services.

Unlike in some other EU countries where workers have to wait for a period before they accrue an entitlement to equal rights, agency workers in Ireland are entitled to equal treatment rights from the first day of placement.

8.5. Checklist of Dos and Don'ts

- Ensure there is clarity in so far as possible as to the actual status of the worker, i.e., whether they are an independent contractor or agency worker, etc.
- Ensure their status is documented to avoid potential disputes about this.
- Ensure requirements of the Protection of Employees (Temporary Agency Work) Act 2012 are complied with.

9. OBLIGATION TO BARGAIN COLLECTIVELY WITH TRADE UNIONS: EMPLOYEES' RIGHT TO STRIKE AND A COMPANY'S RIGHT TO CONTINUE BUSINESS OPERATIONS

9.1. Overview of Union's Right to Organize

The right to form trade unions ('freedom of association') and to bargain collectively with employers are fundamental rights of all people at work.

Historically, the issue of 'union recognition', or collective bargaining with a trade union representing employees, has been a very sensitive one in Ireland. The Constitution is interpreted as prohibiting mandatory union recognition, and against that backdrop, the attempts by the trade union movement to force recognition of unions on Irish employers have had to be dealt with in other ways. The Industrial Relations (Amendment) Act 2015 is the most recent legislative initiative providing for an enhanced and improved framework for collective bargaining in Ireland. For the first time, it provides a definition of what collective bargaining is. It does not provide for mandatory union recognition. The Act provides enhanced protection for workers who may feel that they are being victimized for exercising their rights under the legislation. The Act reinvigorates a framework whereby employers who do not engage in collective bargaining as defined in the Act may be brought before the Labour Court which may then make a binding recommendation in relation to pay and terms and conditions of employment.

Ireland's membership of the EU has also meant that Ireland has transposed legislation that, while sitting easily with our European counterparts, does not sit so easily here. In essence such legislation places obligations upon employers to consult with representatives, rather than the traditional relationship with the employee. This arguably causes huge disquiet to Irish employers, particularly those that are subsidiaries of US corporations. For a variety of reasons, they believe that interacting directly with their workforces, and endeavouring to put in place best-practice terms and conditions, is the commercially better means of controlling and internalizing employment relations issues.

Ireland has implemented the Transnational (Information and Consultation) Directive by way of the Transnational (Information and Consultation) Act 1996 and the European Communities (Transnational Information and Consultation of Employees Act 1996) (Amendment) Regulations 2011 by which multinational organizations must establish European Works Councils (EWC). These are required where the group employs at least 1,000 employees throughout the EU, and there are at least 150 employees in two Member States. Among other provisions, there are requirements in respect of the election of representatives of the workforces to the EWC, and the nature of the information to be furnished by the employer to it, and the degree to which consultation must be engaged in.

Ireland has also implemented the EU Council Directive (2002/14/EC) which provides a general framework for the provision of information to, and consultation with, employees. The Irish transposing legislation is the Employees (Provision of Information and Consultation) Act 2006. A corresponding Code of Practice was introduced by the Irish Government in 2008. The 2006 Act imposes a general obligation on employers to establish arrangements for informing and consulting their employees. This applies to enterprises engaging as few as fifty employees. Employers have the option of initiating the establishment of such structures or waiting for a request from a number of employees.

9.2. Right of Employees to Join Unions

Under Irish constitutional law, employees have the right to join a trade union if that union is willing to accept them into their membership. Employees also have the right not to join a trade union (known as the right to disassociate). This recognition of the right to disassociate is in line with the European Court of Human Rights (ECHR) case law which has developed the 'negative' freedom of association. Despite this, it is permissible for an employer to require that prior to entering into employment, an employee joins a particular trade union with which the employer has a relationship. These are known as 'closed shops' and there are no legislative provisions prohibiting 'closed shops' in this country. However, once an employee is in the employment they cannot be required either to join a trade union or to leave a trade union. Dismissal for trade union activity or membership is automatically unfair and an employee dismissed in such circumstances does not require any particular length of service in order to enforce their rights.

9.3. How Employees Select Unions

Unions are independent of companies. They are usually formed on behalf of a specific sector or industry (e.g., the education or medical sector). Irish employees can join the union of their choice by paying a subscription to this effect. This is determined by the union usually at the rate of 0.5% to 1% of gross salary per year.

9.4. Pre-election Campaigning

Pre-election campaigning is not a feature of the Industrial Relations landscape in Ireland.

9.5. Unfair Labour Practices

Industrial relations legislation gives trade unions a number of immunities that protect them against civil proceedings in relation to unlawful acts (such as interfering with trade or business, conspiracy and inducing breaches of contract) where they have complied with the provisions of the legislation and are acting in contemplation or furtherance of a trade dispute. Employees who engage in strike action are in fundamental breach of their contracts of employment and therefore an employer is entitled to treat participation in strike action as bringing the contract to an end. However, if the employees give their employer proper notice of the strike action and the notice is for a period equivalent to that required to terminate their contracts, then the courts have said that the contract remains suspended during the strike and so there is no breach. Immunities afforded to trade unions are confined to those unions holding negotiation licences from the relevant minister.

The Supreme Court has said that there is an implied term in every contract of employment that employees may lawfully give strike notice and that this notice would suspend the mutual obligations of the parties, that is the obligation on the part of the employee to attend work and the obligation on the employer to pay.

9.6. Relocation of Work/Shutdown of Business

The Terms of Employment (Information) Acts 1994–2014 specifically provide that an employer is obliged to provide an employee with a statement in writing no later than two months after the commencement of employment containing certain particulars in relation to their employment. One of the particulars which must be furnished is the place of work of the employee or alternatively a statement specifying that the employee is required or permitted to work at various places.

In addition to specifying the place of work an employer may seek to incorporate an express relocation or mobility clause in the employee's contract. Such clauses would typically entitle the employer to relocate or move the employee to other offices or branches of the employer within a specified area.

If the contract of employment does not contain a mobility clause, one may be implied by the courts who will consider whether it is reasonable in the circumstances to require the employee to relocate to a given location.

If an employer seeks to relocate or transfer an entire business or part of a business to another location and the employee does not wish to transfer, it is arguable that the employer may be justified in dismissing the employees in question by reason of redundancy. The situation may fall within one of the prescribed grounds for a redundancy as set out in the Redundancy Payments Acts 1967–2014, i.e., that 'the employer has ceased or intends to cease to carry on the business in the place where the employee was employed'.

Cases in relation to relocation and mobility clauses are quite subjective in nature and generally turn on their own specific facts. A common theme running through these cases tends to be the extent to which the employer conducted themselves reasonably.

9.7. Checklist of Dos and Don'ts

- Do not dismiss an employee because of/on the grounds of their membership of a trade union or if that employee has the intention of joining a trade union.
- Do not try to prevent an employee from joining a trade union as it is their constitutional right to do so.
- Ensure mobility clauses are drafted carefully.

10. WORKING CONDITIONS: HOURS OF WORK AND PAYMENT OF WAGES: BY STATUTE OR COLLECTIVE AGREEMENTS

10.1. Overview of Wage and Hours Laws

Working Time in Ireland is governed by the Organisation of Working Time Act 1997. Wage laws are driven by the National Minimum Wage Act 2000 and industry-specific collective agreements such as EROs, REAs and Sectoral Employment Orders (SEOs) (which now operate under a revised legislative framework).

10.2. Hours of Work

The Employment (Miscellaneous Provisions) Act 2018 (the *2018 Act*) aims 'to improve the security and predictability of working hours for employees on insecure contracts and those working variable hours'.

The 2018 Act amends the Organisation of Working Time Act 1997 (as well as amending the Terms of Employment (Information) Acts 1994–2014) and requires employers to provide a written statement to employees outlining their basic terms of employment within five days of commencement. These core terms include hours of work.

As a result of the 2018 Act, employers are no longer able to require employees to be available for work without specific set hours within a contract (except in very limited circumstances). The 2018 Act also introduces the concept of 'banded hours', enabling employees, where their contract does not reflect the hours they have actually worked in the previous twelve months, to request to be placed in a specified 'band' of weekly hours. A 'minimum payment' obligation will also arise where an employer fails to require an employee to work 25% of their contracted hours.

10.3. Minimum Wage

Ireland has a national minimum wage and the current minimum wage for adult workers is EUR 10.50 per hour. The Low Pay Commission makes recommendations to the government annually on the level of national minimum wage. Employments that are subject to EROs or REAs may set out other minimum pay and terms which may be above the minimum wage. A High Court ruling in 2011 stated that EROs were unconstitutional.[7] Following this, the Industrial Relations (Amendment) Act 2012 was introduced to address the constitutional deficiencies identified in this sectoral pay setting mechanism. In 2013, the Supreme Court ruled that REAs established under the Industrial Relations Act 1946 were invalid as there was an impermissible delegation of legislative power involved in their formation.[8] Existing contractual rights of workers in sectors covered by REAs (formed under the 1946 Act) remain unaffected by this ruling as the terms in question were deemed to be implied in their contracts. The Industrial Relations (Amendment) Act 2015 was intended to deal with the deficiencies addressed above. Part 2 of the Industrial Relations (Amendment) Act 2015 provides significant amendments to the REA process in Ireland. It provides for the reintroduction of a mechanism for the registration of employment agreements between an employer or employers and trade unions governing terms and conditions of employment in individual enterprises. It also provides a revised framework to replace the sectoral REAs (now known as SEOs).

10.4. Overtime

Overtime is work done outside normal working hours. There is no statutory obligation in Ireland to pay higher rates such as double time or time and a half for overtime. Industries covered by EROs or REAs may pay higher rates for additional hours worked.

10.5. Meal and Rest Periods

The European Community 'Working Time' Directive applies under Irish law in the form of its transposing legislation The Organisation of Working Time Act 1997 and provides for the following:

7. *John Grace Fried Chicken Limited v. Catering Joint Labour Committee* [2011] IEHC 277.
8. *McGowan and Ors v. Labour Court Ireland and Ors* [2013] IEHC 21.

An employee is entitled to a rest period of not less than 11 consecutive hours in each period of 24 hours during which they work for their employer. The daily rest provision is an entitlement of the employee.

The entitlement to a daily rest period does not apply where:

(i) An employer is, subject to a requirement to provide compensatory rest period(s), permitted to instruct an employee to work for a period in excess of thirteen hours per twenty-four hour period where the worker falls within one of the categories designated in the General Exemption Regulations 1998.
(ii) A collective agreement has been registered by the Labour Court and the agreement provides for compensatory rest.
(iii) There is a change in shift or where work is split up over the day.
(iv) There are exceptional circumstances or an emergency, the consequences of which could not have been avoided despite the exercise of all due care, or there are unusual or unforeseeable circumstances beyond the employer's control.
(v) The work falls under section 3(3) of the Act which enables the Minister to exempt certain categories of workers from specified provisions of the Act, where the 'inherent nature of the activity is such that, if the provision concerned were to apply to a said person, the efficient operation of the service would be adversely affected'. For example, the Organisation of Working Time (Exemption of Civil Protection Services) Regulations 1998 exclude roles such as prison officer, fire officer and customs officer from the application of the daily rest requirements.

An employer cannot require an employee to work for a period of more than four hours and thirty minutes without allowing them a break of at least fifteen minutes (during this four-hour and thirty-minute period). In addition, an employer cannot require an employee to work for a period of more than six hours without allowing them a break of at least thirty minutes (again during this six-hour period). This break may include the fifteen-minute break due after four hours thirty minutes. The break is unpaid.

A break has to take place close to the middle of the work period. Allowing an employee a break at the end of the day is not regarded as satisfying the requirements, while a break too close to the beginning of a shift might be insufficient compliance. Section 13 entitles an employee to an uninterrupted break of thirty-five hours in each period of seven days. It provides that an employee must, in each period of seven days, be granted a rest period of at least twenty-four consecutive hours. This rest period must begin immediately after a daily rest period of eleven hours. The break must, unless the contract states otherwise, include Sunday.

The maximum working week is forty-eight hours, averaged over a period of four months. This reference period is not to include the minimum statutory annual holiday, sick leave or absences under maternity, adoptive, parental, or carer's leave legislation. The averaging period can be increased to six months in particular circumstances or to as much as twelve months (but only in the circumstances where a Collective Agreement is reached between the employer and representatives of employees on behalf of the employees, i.e., trade unions). The Act does provide that this does not apply to 'a person the duration of whose working time . . . is determined by himself or herself …' which might only cover those in very senior management positions such as a Chief Executive Officer (CEO) of a business.

10.6. Deductions from Wages

An employee's salary should be set out in their contract of employment. The amount should be expressed as a gross figure, and the contract should provide for the employer to deduct the Universal Social Charge (USC) Pay As You Earn (PAYE) and PRSI at source. Any other agreed deductions (such as trade union membership dues) should also be specified. The Payment of Wages legislation provides that employers must furnish employees at the time of making payment with details of all deductions. Any other deduction without an employee's consent is unlawful.

Details of all benefits attaching to the employment such as payment to private health insurers in respect of health cover over and above State benefit, etc. should also be set out in detail.

Garnishment

Attachment of earnings is only available in Ireland in the context of maintenance payable to spouses and children. If a parent or spouse fails to comply with a court order in respect of maintenance an attachment of earnings can be sought from the court if the person is in employment. This results in the maintenance amount being deducted at source by the parent's employer.

10.7. Exemptions to Wage and Hour Laws

There are a number of limited exceptions to the National Minimum Wage Act 2000. The Acts do not apply to those employed by a close relative or those doing a statutory apprenticeship. Similarly the provisions of the Organisation of Working Time Act 1997 in relation to rest period and working time do not apply to all employees. They do not apply to the Gardaí, Defence Forces, employees who control their own working hours or family employees on farms or in private homes. The hours of young people are regulated by the Protection of Young Persons (Employment) Act 1996.

There are also separate regulations governing the working time of trainee doctors and employees working at sea. Certain exemptions also apply to those employees employed in transport activities and in certain categories of civil protection.

Child Labour

The employment of young persons in Ireland is governed by the Protection of Young Persons (Employment) Act, 1996. In Irish law, the term 'child worker' is not a recognized term. Instead persons under the age of 18 in employment are divided into two categories 'children' and 'young persons'.

A child is defined as a person who has not reached the age of 16. An employer is not allowed to employ a child to do work subject to a number of exceptions. An employer may employ a child who is over 14 years to do light work during any period outside the school term provided that:

- the hours of work do not exceed seven hours in any day or thirty-five hours in any week;
- the work is not harmful to the safety, health and development of the child; and
- during the period of the summer holidays, the child does not do any work for a period of at least twenty-one days.

An employer may employ a child who is over the age of 15 to do light work during school term time, provided that the hours of work do not exceed eight hours in any week.

A young person is defined as a person who has reached the age of 16 but has not reached the age of 18. An employer is permitted to employ a young person so long as the following conditions are adhered to:

- A young person shall not be required to work more than eight hours in any day or forty hours in any week.
- A young person shall not be employed between the hours of 11 pm and 6 am (provided the day is not before a school day during a school term where such young person is attending school in which case they must finish work by 10 pm). The Minister can make regulations allowing employees under 18 years to work between 11 pm and 7 am the following morning where the Minister is satisfied that there are particular circumstances affecting a particular industry which make it appropriate.
- A young person is afforded a minimum rest period of at least twelve consecutive hours in each twenty-four-hour period.

- A young person must receive a minimum two days rest during a seven-day period, and this rest must be consecutive as far as it is practicable.
- A young person shall not have to work for any period exceeding 4.5 hours without a break of 30 consecutive minutes. There is no entitlement to payment for this break.

Where an employer decides to employ a child or young person it is obliged to obtain a copy of the prospective employee's birth certificate or some other 'satisfactory' evidence of their age before the young person commences employment. Before employing a child the employer is required to obtain the written permission of the parent or guardian of the child. The employer is also required to keep a register of young persons in their employment which must detail full names, date of birth, place of birth, starting times, finishing times, rates of pay and total remuneration paid to each young person in question.

10.8. Recordkeeping Requirements

10.8.1. Information That Must Be Maintained

There are detailed requirements in relation to information regarding hour and wage laws which must be maintained under Irish law.

Under the Payment of Wages Act 1991, employees are entitled to a written statement showing the gross amount of wages and the nature and amount of any deduction therefrom.

Under the Organisation of Working Time Act 1997, an employer must keep records to demonstrate compliance with the provisions of the Act. Section 25 of the Act is expanded upon by the implementation of the Organisation of Working Time (Records) (Prescribed Form and Exemption) Regulations 2001 which details specifically the following records which must be kept:

- the name and address of each employee, their Personal Public Service (PPS) number and their job description;
- a copy of the statement provided to each employee in accordance with the Terms of Employment (Information) Act 1994;
- the days and total hours worked in each week by each employee;
- any days and hours of leave in a week granted by way of annual leave or in respect of a public holiday to each employee and the payment made to each employee in respect of that leave;
- any additional days pay in respect of a public holiday; and
- in certain cases, details of rest breaks taken by employees.

If there are no clocking-in facilities provided in the particular workplace, a form must be provided to record the days and hours worked in each week by each employee in the form of OWT1 or in a form to like effect.

Under the Protection of Employees (Young Persons) Act 1996, an employer who employs young persons must maintain the following records for at least three years:

- Prior to employing a young person or child, the employer must obtain a copy of the birth certificate or other satisfactory evidence of the age of the young person or child.
- Before employing the child, the employer must obtain the written permission of the parent or guardian of the child.

Under the Protection of Employees (Young Persons) Act 1996 an employer must maintain a register or other satisfactory record in relation to every young person or child employed by the employer with the following details:

- their full name;
- their date of birth;
- the time they commence work each day;
- the day they finish work each day;
- the rate of wages or salary paid to them for their normal working hours each day, week, month or year as appropriate;
- the total amount paid to each young person or child by way of wages or salary;
- the employer must display the prescribed abstract of the Act at the employer's place of work in such a prominent place where employees under 18 years of age may easily read it;
- the employer must give employees under 18 years of age a copy of the official summary of the Act.

In light of the GDPR, employers must be aware of their responsibilities regarding the obtaining, controlling and processing of personal. The definition of 'personal data' under the GDPR and the Data Protection Act 2018 is broad, and certainly includes some of the above-mentioned data, including names and addresses of employees, PPS numbers and job descriptions. Any retention of personal data should be in line with the Data Protection Act 2018.

10.8.2. Records That Must Be Retained

Under the National Minimum Wage Act 2000, employers must keep at the premises or place where an employee works such records as are necessary to demonstrate compliance with the provisions of the Act. The employer must retain these records for three years from the date of their making.

Under the Organisation of Working Time Acts 1997 records must be kept for at least three years from the date of their making.

Under the Payment of Wages Act 1991 it is advisable that records are kept for up to six years.

10.8.3. Failure to Maintain Required Records

Failure to maintain the records in accordance with the above legislative requirements can trigger fines and/or criminal sanctions.

10.9. Reductions in Compensation Caused by Economic Downturn

When economic conditions suffer a downturn an employer may have to look at short-term measures of reducing their wage cost without reducing headcount. Two ways an employer can do this is by introducing short-time working or lay-off. Short-time working arises where due to a reduction in the amount of work to be done an employee's pay or hours are less than half the normal amount due. An employer must notify the employee before the reduction occurs. The employer should keep the employee apprised of the situation. The short time must be temporary in nature. A lay-off arises where the employer is unable to provide work at all for a short period. A right to claim redundancy usually arises where an employee is on lay-off or short time for a period of four or more consecutive weeks over a period of six or more weeks within a period of thirteen consecutive weeks.

10.10. Checklist of Dos and Don'ts

- Ensure that employees are afforded the relevant breaks and rest periods in compliance with the provisions of the Organisation of Working Time Act 1997.
- Ensure that the appropriate statements/documentation to vouch for compliance with the Payment of Wages Act 1991 are given to employees.
- Ensure the minimum wage is given to all employees. Employers are obviously free to set higher rates of remuneration, however, this is the basic minimum which must be complied with.
- Ensure appropriate records demonstrating compliance with the above and data protection legislation are maintained.

11. OTHER WORKING CONDITIONS AND BENEFITS: BY STATUTE, COLLECTIVE AGREEMENTS OR COMPANY POLICY

11.1. Health and Other Insurance

One of the most common benefits offered by employers is access to a private health insurance scheme. This means that the cost may be reduced for the employee (however, it will still be taxed). There is no obligation on an employer to offer or make available health insurance, but many employers do so.

11.2. Pension and Retirement Benefits

Subject to any commitments regarding pensions in the contract of employment, there is no obligation on an employer to establish a pension scheme. However, employers who do not operate a pension scheme (or who operate a pension scheme and impose a waiting period of admission in excess of six months' service) are required under Part X of the Pensions Act, 1990 to provide access to a standard PRSA (Personal Retirement Savings Account).

A PRSA is a contract between an employee and an authorized PRSA provider in the form of an investment account. There is no obligation on the employer to contribute to a PRSA. However, the employer must ensure that the PRSA is an approved standard PRSA and must also:

(i) Inform excluded employees that they have a right to contribute to a standard PRSA.
(ii) Provide access to financial advice and paid time off to obtain this advice.
(iii) Deduct and remit contributions on behalf of the employee to the PRSA.
(iv) Provide a statement to the employee each month detailing deductions.

11.3. Vacation and Holiday Payments on Termination

Employees who meet the qualifying criteria in relation to time worked must be allowed twenty paid working days' leave in respect of a period of twelve months. Holidays may only be taken at times agreed with the employer. The employer has to, among other matters, take account of the opportunities for rest and relaxation available to an employee.

In addition to annual holidays, there are ten public holidays in Ireland (New Year's Day, the first Monday in February or 1 February if the date falls on a Friday, St. Patrick's Day, Easter Monday, the first Monday in May, the first Monday in June, the first Monday in August, the last Monday in October, Christmas Day, and St. Stephen's Day). In respect of public holidays, an employee must be given a paid day off on that day, or a paid day off within a month of the day, or an extra day's annual leave, or an extra day's pay, all of which are at the option of the employer.

The Organisation of Working Time Act 1997 was amended by section 86 of the Workplace Relations Act in 2015 to allow for the accrual of statutory annual leave when a worker is on long-term certified sick leave. The amendment means that workers who have been sick during a leave year and were not able to take their annual leave entitlement are able to take such accrued annual leave within a fifteen-month period after the end of the relevant leave year. This brings Irish law in line with developments from the 'CJEU'.

11.4. Leaves of Absence

11.4.1. Personal Leave

An employee can take unpaid personal leave if an employer agrees to this.

11.4.2. Medical or Sick Leave

There is currently no statutory entitlement to sick pay in Ireland. The contract should set out the procedures in relation to absence due to illness. Except in employments regulated by an ERO or REA, there is no obligation upon employers to pay employees during such absence. However, by virtue of the payment of PRSI contributions, employees may have an entitlement to certain social welfare benefits. Many employers continue to pay employees during short absences grounded on illness. It is usual to provide that a certificate from a doctor be furnished by the employee in respect of absences of more than two days. Employees may qualify for state illness benefit – no payment is made for the first three days of illness (known as waiting days). Employers may require the employee in respect of absences of more than three days to apply for the appropriate social welfare benefit and to pay that benefit to the employer who will continue to pay the employee in full during the absence.

Some employers, in relation to long-term illnesses, take out what is known as Permanent Health Insurance (PHI) to cover payment of part of the income of employees who suffer from long-term illnesses.

In light of disability discrimination legislation, caution must be exercised if consideration is being given to disciplining employees in the case of absence due to illness.

11.4.3. Bereavement Leave

Leave may be granted to an employee in the case of death of a family member or close friend. There is no legal entitlement to compassionate leave. It is often included in the company handbook in which case it may become a contractual entitlement. A typical example is two to four days' leave being granted (this may either be paid or unpaid). Alternatively it is something that may be granted by the employer on an ad hoc basis.

11.4.4. Family Leave

An employee who is the parent or acting in loco parentis of a child is entitled to leave from their employment, for a period of twenty-six working weeks, to enable them to take care of the child. This is known as parental leave. The entitlement generally applies to employees who have one year of continuous employment with the employer and usually applies only in respect of children under 12 years of age. It can be extended to 16 where the child is disabled or suffers from a long-term illness. Employees returning from parental leave have the right to request a change to their working patterns/hours or both for a fixed period on their return. Employers do not have to grant this request but must consider it.[9]

The purpose of parental leave is to 'take care of the child'. Accordingly disciplinary action may be taken by employers against employees who are found to be abusing this. An employer cannot refuse this leave entirely. An employer can only postpone it for up to six months and even then only because granting the leave would have a 'substantial adverse effect' on the business. This is a high threshold for businesses to prove. It would probably be more conceivable that small businesses would be able to surmount this threshold by showing that the absence of a key employee could have such an adverse effect. It would be more difficult for a large enterprise to prove that they would be unable to do without one employee for what is a relatively short period of time.

9. European Union (Parental Leave) Regulations 2013.

Employees are entitled to leave, with pay, from their employment for urgent family reasons (force majeure leave) where sickness or accident makes the immediate presence of the employee indispensable. By its very nature, notice cannot be given for this type of leave, but the employee is obliged as soon as reasonably practicable to give written notice to the employer of the date on which leave was taken and give a statement of facts as to why it was taken. It may be taken in respect of the following people: a child, a spouse or person with whom the employee is living in a relationship of domestic dependency, a person to whom the employee is in loco parentis, a brother or sister, a parent or grandparent. Force majeure leave is restricted to three days in any period of twelve consecutive months or five days in any period of thirty-six consecutive months.

Under the Carer's Leave Act 2001, employees can also take temporary unpaid leave to personally care for a person who requires full-time care and attention. An employee who has a minimum of one years' service is entitled to take up to 104 weeks' leave. The minimum amount of time an employee can take is thirteen weeks. At the end of the carer's leave, if reasonably practicable an employee is entitled to return to their job on the same terms and conditions that they had prior to taking the leave.

Parent's Leave is a period of five-weeks leave available to each parent during the first two years of a child's life or adoption. A parent's benefit is available from the Government in respect of this period.

The Paternity Leave and Benefits Act 2016 provides for two continuous weeks' leave to a 'relevant parent'. Paternity benefit is available from the Government in respect of this period.

11.4.5. Pregnancy Leave

Where working conditions pose a potential risk to a pregnant employee an employer is obliged to conduct a 'risk assessment'. If as a result it is felt the employee's health may be at risk they are eligible for a period of paid 'Health & Safety' leave. Pregnant employees are entitled to time off work with pay to attend antenatal classes (other than the last three classes in such a set). They are also entitled to time off without loss of pay (on production of appropriate vouching documentation) to attend antenatal appointments.

11.4.6. Maternity Leave

Female employees are entitled by law to twenty-six weeks' leave in respect of maternity. This may be extended, at the employee's election, by a further period of sixteen weeks. There is no qualifying period of service before an employee can take maternity leave.

Employees are required to notify their employers in writing of their intention to take maternity leave not later than four weeks before the commencement of maternity leave. Employees must also produce a medical or other appropriate certificate confirming the pregnancy and specifying the expected week of confinement (the date that they are due to give birth) at the same time. This is a mandatory requirement under section 9 of the Maternity Protection Act 1994 as amended by the 2004 Act.

With the exception of the right to pay, all other employment rights are preserved during the maternity and/or additional maternity leave period. Some employers may continue to pay their employees while they are on maternity leave but that is a contractual matter only and may be subject to conditions such as a twelve-month minimum service period before the leave is taken. During the maternity leave period there may be an entitlement to social welfare or statutory maternity benefit. Continuity of service and entitlement to annual leave including public holidays are all preserved while on maternity and/or additional maternity leave.

Termination of an individual's contract of employment while they are absent from work on maternity leave, additional maternity leave, pregnancy-related health and safety leave, during a period of ante- or postnatal care or during the period that they are still breastfeeding in accordance with the breastfeeding regulations is void. Any notice of termination served during any of these periods is also void.

If a notice of termination of employment is given to an employee before that employee has served notice of their intention to take maternity leave, and this notice of termination is due to expire during the employee's absence from work or during a period of ante- or postnatal care or during the period that they are still breastfeeding, then the notice is extended by this period.

Employees have the right to return to work with the same employer for whom they were working prior to the start of their leave. In the case of a change of ownership of an undertaking, employees have a right to work with the new employer in the job they held immediately before the start of their maternity leave under terms and conditions not less favourable than those which would have been applicable to the employee had they not been absent from work.

Where it is not reasonably practicable for the employer or its successor to permit the employee to return to work in the same position and under the same terms and conditions of employment, the employee is entitled to be offered suitable alternative work by the employer under a new contract of employment, the terms of which are not less favourable to the employee than those of their previous contract.

Entitlement to return to work or to be offered suitable alternative work is subject to an employee, not later than four weeks before the date on which they expect to return to work, notifying their employer in writing of their intention to return to work and the date on which they expect to return.

Where a bonus payment is made for work performed in the course of the year then it should be pro-rated. In order to make a decision on entitlement to a bonus, employers need to consider the precise detail and terms of the bonus scheme, as well as past practice, and the possibility of discrimination before taking a decision to pay or withhold a bonus payment.

Similar leave provisions apply in circumstances of adoption.

11.4.7. Injury at Work

If an employee has an accident at work, they may apply for Injury Benefit. This is a weekly State payment if they are unfit for work due to an accident at work or an occupational illness. Redress for an injury at work caused by an employer's negligence is made through the Personal Injuries Assessment Board. Health and Safety legislation sets out an employers' obligation to provide a safe workplace.

11.5. Checklist of Dos and Don'ts

- Do not discriminate against an employee who has an illness/disability, or where an employee exercises their rights under the Acts which provide for family leave.
- Particular care must be taken when dealing with pregnant employees to ensure they are afforded a high level of protection set down in the legislation.
- Ensure requests for any kind of leave are appropriately documented and records maintained.

12. WORKERS' COMPENSATION

12.1. Overview

If an employee is involved in an accident at work then they may be entitled to compensation. One of the means of obtaining compensation is by making a claim to the Personal Injuries Assessment Board. All claims, including workplace accidents (employer liability cases) must be submitted to the Personal Injuries Assessment Board before commencing proceedings. The employee will be entitled to compensation if they can prove that the injury was the fault of the employer or another employee (for whom the employer is vicariously liable). An employee can claim for the injuries suffered, medical costs and loss of earnings.

12.2. Checklist of Dos and Don'ts

- Notify insurers once a notice of a claim has been received.

13. COMPANY'S OBLIGATION TO PROVIDE SAFE AND HEALTHY WORKPLACE

13.1. Overview of Safety and Environmental Laws and Regulations

The main legislation providing for the health and safety of people in the workplace is the Safety, Health and Welfare at Work Act 2005.

There are also a significant number of regulations that apply to places of work within Ireland which provide more details of the regulatory requirements under primary legislation (the Acts). The most significant regulation is the Safety, Health and Welfare at Work (General Application) Regulations, 2007 which contain many of the provisions that apply to almost all workplaces.

In addition to legislation there are a number of 'Codes of Practice' that also relate to health and safety in the workplace. These Codes while not legally binding are viewed as best practice within the industry and may be taken into account where there is a claim.

13.2. Requirements

Under the Safety, Health and Welfare at Work Act 2005 every employer is required to carry out a risk assessment for the workplace which should identify any hazards present in the workplace, assess the risks arising from such hazards and identify the steps to be taken to deal with any risks.

The employer must also prepare a safety statement which is based on the risk assessment. The statement should also contain the details of people in the workforce who are responsible for safety issues. Employees should be given access to this statement and employers should review it on a regular basis. The Health and Safety Authority has published guidelines on risk assessments and safety statements.

13.3. Rights of Employees

Pursuant to the Safety, Health and Welfare at Work Act 2005, every employee including fixed-term employees and temporary employees are entitled to a safe workplace which uses safe plant and equipment. Employees are entitled to training and instruction on health and safety issues, and they also have the right to be protected from any behaviour or improper conduct likely to put their safety, health or welfare at risk.

Employees have the right to inspect any safety statement which is based on an assessment and identification of any hazard in the workplace. The statement must set out the preventative and protective measures taken to protect employees by setting out the policies and procedures that will be followed and provide for the election of a safety representative in the workplace and emphasizes consultation with the workers.

13.4. Rights of Employer

Employees must take reasonable care to protect the health and safety of themselves and of other people in the workplace. They must not engage in improper behaviour that will endanger themselves or others and must ensure that they are not under the influence of any intoxicant to the extent that they could be a danger to themselves or others while at work.

Employers have the right to request that an employee undergo any reasonable medical or other assessment.

Employees have reporting duties. They must inform their employer or supervisor without delay of any defects in the place of work or equipment which might be a danger to health and safety.

13.5. Specific Standards

The employer should tell employees about any risks that require the wearing of protective equipment. The employer should provide protective equipment (such as protective clothing, headgear, footwear, eyewear, gloves) together with training on how to use it, where necessary. An employee is under a duty to take reasonable care for their own safety and to use any protective equipment supplied. The protective equipment should be provided free of charge to employees if it is intended for use at the workplace only. Usually, employees should be provided with their own personal equipment.

There is a range of measures that employers must take in regard to Visual Display Units (VDUs). These include examining the reflection and glare, the operator's position in front of the VDU, the keyboard and the software used.

Operators must be given adequate breaks from the VDU. In addition, employers must arrange for eye tests and, if required, make a contribution towards the purchase of prescription eyeglasses.

13.6. Injury or Accident at Work

All accidents in the workplace should be reported to the employer, who should record the details of the incident. Reporting the accident will help to safeguard social welfare and other rights which may arise as a result of an occupational accident. An employer is obliged to report any accident that results in an employee missing three consecutive days at work (not including the day of the accident) to the Health and Safety Authority.

13.7. Workplace Violence

The possibility of violence towards employees in the workplace tends to be covered in the safety statement. Proper safeguards should be put into place to eliminate the risk of violence as far as possible, and the employee should be provided with appropriate means of minimizing the remaining risk.

13.8. Fines and Penalties

The Courts may impose fines or prison sentences or both, depending on the seriousness of the offence. Most offences including any breaches of Regulations under the Safety, Health and Welfare at Work Act 2005 may be tried either in the District Court, where the maximum penalty is EUR 3,000 per charge and/or up to six months' imprisonment, or on indictment in the Circuit Court where the maximum penalty is EUR 3,000,000 and/or imprisonment for a term not exceeding two years.

13.9. Checklists of Dos and Don'ts

– Identify the hazards and assess the risks that may be present in the workplace.
– Draw up a document (safety statement) which sets out an action programme for safeguarding the safety, health and welfare of employees while they are at work.
– Permit employees to select a safety representative and consult with either the employees directly or their safety representative(s) (or both) on any

proposed measures likely to substantially affect their safety, health, or welfare at work.
- Do not penalize any employee for acting in accordance with safety and health laws or for reporting complaints regarding safety and health matters at work.

14. IMMIGRATION, SECONDMENT AND FOREIGN ASSIGNMENT

14.1. Overview Laws Controlling Immigration

Citizens of European countries, the European Economic Area (EEA) and Switzerland benefit from provisions relating to the free movement of workers in Europe pursuant to Article 45 of the Treaty on the Functioning of the European Union.

In general, non-EEA nationals must have a permit to work in Ireland. The Employment Permits (Amendment) Act 2014 aims at streamlining and updating the permit system, especially for inward investors. It also addresses the lack of access to employment rights for undocumented workers. The Act has replaced the five principal employment permits with an extensive list of nine new permits. The Act has addressed the difficulties identified by Judge Hogan in the High Court case of *Hussein v. The Labour Court and Ors* [2012] IEHC 364 and finally provides a defence to employees who have taken up employment without an employment permit, where it can be proved that the foreign national took all reasonable steps to ensure compliance with the section.

In order to further deter employers from employing foreign nationals without a work permit, there is a new provision allowing the foreign national to take civil action for compensation against their employer, notwithstanding the illegality of the contract.

14.2. Recruiting, Screening and Hiring Process

The Act retains the Labour Market Needs Test and extends the requirement for a Labour Market Test to all new applications, regardless of the applicant, for General Employment Permits and Contract for Services Employment Permits with certain grounds for waiver which include:

- where employment is one included on the Critical Skills Occupations list;
- where annual remuneration is a minimum of EUR 64,000;[10]

10. Employment permits cannot be issued in respect of employments, irrespective of remuneration, on the ineligible categories of employment for an employment permit list.

- where application has been recommended by an Enterprise Development Agency (such as IDA Ireland);
- in the case of a former General Employment permit holder who has been made redundant in the previous six months;
- where a General Employment Permit application is in respect of a career with a proven history of caring for the sick person.

One of the most notable and applauded changes introduced by the 2014 Act in relation to eligibility criteria is the waiving of the 50:50 Rule for start-ups with enterprise agency support from the likes of IDA Ireland or Enterprise Ireland. The 50:50 Rule requires employers seeking to hire foreign nationals on an employment permit to have at least 50% of their workforce from the EEA.

This is a particularly difficult rule for start-ups to meet and so this change helpfully addresses the reality faced by these businesses. Such start-ups must comply with 50:50 Rule within two years of the first employment permit being issued.

Also, the Act formally confirms that the Department of Enterprise, Trade and Employment may have regard to the recommendations of IDA Ireland and Enterprise Ireland when processing applications.

14.3. Obligations of Employer to Enforce Immigration Laws

Employers who wish to employ people who need employment permits have to meet certain requirements. They must be legally trading in Ireland – this means they must be registered with the Revenue Commissioners and with the Companies Registration Office (CRO) if the employer is a company.

The employer must employ the person directly – this means that applications from recruitment agencies, agents, intermediaries or companies who intend to outsource or subcontract the applicant to work in another company are not accepted.

There is a limit to the proportion of the workforce who can be employment permit holders. Employees who have employment permits are obliged to abide by the immigration rules. This means that they may need a visa in order to come here and they must register with the immigration authorities. Once an employment permit has been granted to an employee, an employer may not transfer this permit to another employee or use it to employ a foreign national other than the foreign national to whom the permit was granted.

The Employment Permits Acts address the obligations incumbent on employers and provides that a person shall not employ a non-national in the State except in accordance with an employment permit. A breach of this constitutes a criminal offence. Consequently, employers should ensure that appropriate employment permit records are maintained and all relevant documentation submitted to the Department of Enterprise, Trade and Employment to ensure that non-national employees are compliant with the requirements under the Employment Permits Acts.

14.4. Fines and Penalties

Depending on the offence committed, an employer and/or an employee may be fined from between EUR 3,000 and EUR 250,000. Prison sentences ranging from twelve months up to ten years may also be imposed.

14.5. Secondment/Foreign Assignment

In Ireland, there is the Intra-Company Transfer Employment Permit which is designed to facilitate the transfer of senior management, key personnel or trainees who are foreign nationals from an overseas branch of a multinational corporation to its Irish branch. However, it cannot be used to permanently substitute the filling of a vacancy which otherwise would have resulted in a job opportunity for the labour market.

Furthermore, in relation to employees remaining on a foreign payroll, the Department of, Enterprise, Trade and Employment preference is for all Employment Permit holders to be employed, salaried and paid under an Irish Employment contract. It therefore applies strict criteria in situations where employees remain employed by a foreign-based employer.

Before granting an Intra-Company Employment Permit, the Department of Enterprise, Trade and Employment examine a number of different criteria relating to both the employer and the prospective employee.

14.6. Checklist of Dos and Don'ts

- Foreign nationals who are legally working in Ireland must be afforded exactly the same rights under employment legislation as Irish nationals working in Ireland.
- Employers must ensure that a foreign national has the appropriate employment permit before commencing work.
- Employers must carry out a labour market needs test before applying for a general employment permit or a contract for services employment permit for a prospective employee.

15. RESTRICTIVE COVENANTS AND PROTECTION OF TRADE SECRETS AND CONFIDENTIAL INFORMATION

15.1. Overview

Irrespective of whether it is expressly set out in the contract, all employees are bound by common law to keep confidential all matters relating to their employment. Nevertheless, the obligation that continues both during and after employment should be set out in the contract. Provisions should also be included for the return of confidential information in whatever form, at the end of employment.

15.2. The Law of Trade Secrets

The common law will restrain an employee from using trade secrets, even where there are no written contractual restrictions. In the leading UK case of *Faccenda Chicken Limited v. Fowler*[11] the Court of Appeal held that in the absence of an express term in an employment contract the obligations of an employee in respect of the use and disclosure of information are the subject of implied terms. At the end of the contract, the onus not to use or disclose the information covers only information that contains a sufficiently high level of confidentiality so as to amount to a trade secret. The difficulty, however, relates to defining what exactly constitutes confidential information and trade secrets. It is not always easy to distinguish general know-how or information that one acquires from just being present in a business from specific employer information. The leading UK case referred to above is authority for the proposition that matters which should be categorized as trade secrets, or should be known to an employee as such, will have the benefit of protection when the employment relationship ends, even where an employer has not specifically brought to the attention of the employee the exact boundaries of what he seeks to classify and protect as confidential. Intellectual property law has also been relatively successful in protecting inventions and trademarks.

15.3. Restrictive Covenants and Non-compete Agreements

While it is usual in many contracts to provide restrictions in respect of an employee's ability to compete after the employment, significant difficulty can be encountered in enforcing such provisions. While detailed advice

11. *Faccenda Chicken Limited v. Fowler* [1986] IRLR 69.

should be taken on the drafting of all such provisions for the particular circumstances, employers should note that there is an overriding obligation upon them to be able to justify the need to restrain an employee's ability to compete after employment. Subject to satisfying that, the terms of the restrictions should be in the narrowest possible terms required to protect that vital interest. The length of time of the restraint, the geographic area over which it extends, and the nature of the businesses or products and services from which the employee is to be restrained, should not be excessive as that will only increase the risk of non-enforceability. Recently, however, the Irish courts have shown an increased willingness to consider the circumstances in which non-compete clauses might be upheld in order to protect the legitimate business interests of the employer. The courts have made it clear that there must be an identifiable business interest at stake and the contractual restriction must be clear and reasonable in terms of geographical scope, duration and the nature of the business activity involved. Non-solicitation and non-dealing clauses are generally easier to enforce.

15.4. Protection of Trade Secrets Regulations

The EU (Protection of Secrets) Regulations 2018, which implements EU Directive 2016/943, puts the definition of 'trade secrets' on a statutory footing for the first time in Ireland. The 2018 Regulations provides for remedies in the event a trade secret is unlawfully acquired, used or disclosed. The Regulations ensure the confidentiality of the trade secret during court proceedings by limiting access to the hearing and court documents containing the trade secret. In the event of an unlawful disclosure, the owner of the trade secret has six years to take action. The infringer may be subject to orders including the destruction of infringing goods, injunctive measures and/or damages. Criminal sanctions including fines of up to EUR 50,000 or imprisonment of up to three years are also provided for.

15.5. Checklist of Dos and Don'ts

- Ensure any restrictive covenant is drafted appropriately for the business concerned.
- Outline in the contract in so far as possible what might be considered confidential information and trade secrets.

16. PROTECTION OF WHISTLE-BLOWING CLAIMS

16.1. Overview

The Protected Disclosures Act 2014 protects workers in all sectors. In accordance with international best practice, the safeguards in the Act are extended to a wide range of 'workers'. The concept of 'worker' includes employees (public and private sector), contractors, trainees, agency staff, former employees and interns and members of An Garda Síochána.

'Protected disclosure' means the disclosure of relevant information, which in the reasonable belief of the worker tends to show one or more relevant wrongdoings and came to the attention of the worker in connection with their employment.

'Relevant wrongdoings' are defined in an exhaustive list and include the following:

- the commission of an offence;
- a miscarriage of justice;
- non-compliance with a legal obligation;
- health and safety threats;
- misuse of public monies;
- mismanagement by a public official;
- damage to the environment; or
- concealment or destruction of information relating to any of the foregoing.

The motivation for making the disclosure is irrelevant. The UK experience showed that maintaining a requirement to make a disclosure in good faith led to significant obstacles, impeding the effective working of the regime. In its place, there is a provision allowing for the reduction of compensation payable under the Act to be reduced by up to 25% where the investigation of the relevant wrongdoing concerned was not the only or main motivation for the making of the disclosure.

The Act provides for a tiered disclosure regime with a number of avenues open to workers. The Act encourages the vast majority of disclosures to be made to the employer in the first instance. However, other options are available where this is inappropriate or impossible.

16.1.1. Internal Disclosure to an Employer or Other Responsible Person

A worker may make a protected disclosure to their employer where they reasonably believe that the information shows or tends to show a 'relevant wrongdoing' connected with the worker's employment. Where the worker reasonably believes that the wrongdoing relates to the conduct of some person other than their employer, or to something for which some other person has legal responsibility, then the disclosure can be made to that person.

16.1.2. Disclosure to a Prescribed Person

The Minister for Public Expenditure and Reform has prescribed a wide list of 'prescribed persons' (e.g., a regulatory body) whose roles and responsibilities are defined by law and are prescribed to receive certain disclosures of relevant wrongdoings. [12] Where a worker chooses to disclose in this manner they must reasonably believe the information disclosed and any allegation contained in it to be substantially true.

16.1.3. Minister

A worker employed in a public body may make a protected disclosure to the sponsoring Department rather than to their employer.

16.1.4. Legal Advisor

A disclosure made in the course of obtaining legal advice from a barrister, solicitor, trade union or an official of an excepted body is protected.

16.1.5. Other Disclosures

There is also provision for disclosure in other circumstances, i.e., disclosure potentially into the public domain (such as the media) where the standard for reporting is significantly higher. In order for this type of disclosure to be protected the worker must:

- reasonably believe that the information disclosed is substantially true;
- that the disclosure is not made for personal gain; and
- the making of the disclosure is in all the circumstances reasonable.

In addition, one or more of the following conditions must be met:

12. *See* the Protected Disclosures Act 2014 (Disclosure to Prescribed Persons) Order 2020.

- at the time of making the disclosure the worker reasonably believes that they will be subject to penalization and detriment by their employer if the disclosure is made to the employer;
- in a case where there is no prescribed person in relation to the relevant wrongdoing, the worker reasonably believes that evidence will be destroyed/concealed if a disclosure is made to the employer;
- the worker has previously made a disclosure of substantially the same nature to either their employer or prescribed person and no action was taken; and
- the relevant wrongdoing is of an exceptionally serious nature.

In determining whether this disclosure is in all the circumstances reasonable, regard shall be had to a number of factors including the identity of the person to whom the disclosure is made, the seriousness of the relevant wrongdoing, whether the wrongdoing is continuing or likely to occur in the future and whether disclosure is made in breach of a duty of confidentiality.

The Act provides whistle-blowers with the following specific protections:

- protection from dismissal for having made a protected disclosure;
- the employee can be awarded compensation of up to five years' remuneration for unfair dismissal on the grounds of having made a protected disclosure; this is in stark contrast to the two years' remuneration available under the existing statutory unfair dismissals regime; also, an employee who claims to have been dismissed or threatened with dismissal for having made a protected disclosure can apply to the Circuit Court for relief pending the determination or settlement of an unfair dismissal claim and the Court may re-engagement of an employee or payment of salary pending a hearing;
- protection from penalization by the employer;
- civil immunity from action for damages and a qualified privilege under defamation law;
- a right of action in tort where a whistle-blower or a member of their family experiences coercion, intimidation, harassment or discrimination at the hands of a third party;
- protection of their identity (subject to certain exceptions); and
- it will not be a criminal offence to make a whistle-blowing report which is a protected disclosure under the Act.

The Act includes measures to protect the identity of whistle-blowers to ensure that any disclosures made are treated confidentially. The default position is therefore not to disclose the identity. However, there are certain exceptions to this set out in the Act.

16.2. Checklist of Dos and Don'ts

- Public sector bodies are obliged to establish and publish policies and procedures to deal with whistle-blowing.
- All other employers should put whistle-blowing policies in place so as to ensure they are in a position to meet the requirements of the legislation and encourage workers to come forward to them in the first instance if they wish to make a protected disclosure.

17. PROHIBITION OF DISCRIMINATION IN THE WORKPLACE

17.1. Overview of Anti-discrimination Laws

Ireland has implemented very wide ranging discrimination legislation that outlaws harassment, sexual harassment and victimization of employees by reference to the following characteristics:

(i) gender;
(ii) civil status;
(iii) family status (the responsibilities that an employee has as a parent or primary career);
(iv) sexual orientation;
(v) religion;
(vi) age;
(vii) disability;
(viii) race (including colour, nationality or ethnic/national origin); and
(ix) membership of the Traveller Community, which means membership of a community of people who are commonly called Travellers and who are identified (both by themselves and others) as people with a shared history, culture and traditions including, historically, a nomadic way of life on the island of Ireland.

The Employment Equality Acts 1998–2015 protect all classes of employees from discriminatory treatment, including full-time, part-time and fixed-term employees in the public and private sectors, agency workers, partners in partnerships and self-employed contractors. The Acts also prohibit discrimination by an employer against an employee or prospective employee with respect to: access to employment; conditions of employment; training or experience for or in relation to employment; promotion; or regrading or classification of posts. Unlike the Unfair Dismissals Acts, there is no service requirement for an employee disputing a dismissal where it is alleged there is an employment equality issue. Both direct and indirect discriminations are prohibited, although indirect discrimination is not unlawful when it can be objectively justified by a legitimate reason, and the means of achieving that reason are appropriate and necessary.

Remedies include compensation for discriminatory dismissal and discrimination of up to two years' remuneration.

Complaints are heard in the first instance by an Adjudication Officer in the WRC or may be heard by the Circuit Court with respect to gender-based pay discrimination claims. The WRC can make the following orders:

(i) payment of arrears of remuneration for up to three years prior to the date of the referral;
(ii) an order for compensation as a result of acts of discrimination or victimization, not exceeding two years of gross remuneration;
(iii) unlimited compensation for discrimination on the gender ground (where it is referred directly to the Circuit Court);
(iv) an order for equal treatment;
(v) an order that the addressees of the order take a specified course of action; or
(vi) an order for reinstatement or re-engagement with or without an order for compensation.

17.2. Age Discrimination

There has been an increase in age discrimination cases in Ireland in recent years.

Age discrimination applies not only to older workers but also to younger workers. It is unlawful to advertise a job in such a way that the advertisement could reasonably be interpreted as indicating an intention to discriminate. It is no longer possible to advertise for a 'young and dynamic professional'. There are many express exceptions to the prohibition on discrimination on the grounds of age contained in both European and Irish legislation.

It does not constitute discrimination on the age ground to set a maximum age for recruitment which takes account of any cost or period of time involving or training a recruit to a standard at which the recruit will be effective in that job, and the need for there to be a reasonable period of time prior to retirement age during which the recruit will be effective in that job. This is a limited exception and should be used advisedly.

At the other end of the life cycle of a worker there is no overall national retirement age set out in Irish legislation. However, the usual retirement age in Ireland is 65 but this may change as entitlement to the State pension rose to 66 in 2014. If an employer wishes to have a retirement age this should be inserted into the contract of employment. Ireland's Employment Equality

Acts expressly allow employers to fix a compulsory retirement age for staff without triggering age discrimination claims. However, in the wake of a number of conflicting European and national decisions on this point, the Equality (Miscellaneous Provisions) Act 2015 confirmed that employers can only impose a mandatory retirement age on staff where it can be objectively justified.

To reach this threshold: (i) a mandatory retirement age must be objectively and reasonably justified by reference to a legitimate aim; and (ii) the means of achieving that aim must be appropriate and necessary.

This brings the Irish legislation in line with the grounding EU Directive and case law on this point. One of the consequences of the new law is that if fixed-term contracts are offered post-retirement, the employer will have to demonstrate evidence of objective justification for the termination of employment at the point of expiry of the fixed-term contract. Guidance in this area has been recently provided by the WRC and the Irish Human Rights and Equality Commission.

17.3. Race Discrimination

As a result of Ireland's increasingly multicultural society, claims on the grounds of racial discrimination are on the rise. These claims are, however, difficult to prove as motivation for racial comment/action is often quite covert and on occasion the perpetrator may not even be aware that the conduct/verbal language used is racist. As a result obtaining direct evidence of discrimination on the grounds of race can be difficult and a decision often has to be made whether or not an inference of discrimination on the grounds of race can be determined on the facts.

17.4. Sex Discrimination/Sexual Harassment

Gender/Sex discrimination is one of the prohibited grounds. Claims under this heading tend to relate in the main to claims for equal pay and claims relating to pregnancy/maternity issues. In very basic terms gender discrimination prohibits discrimination on the basis that one is a man and the other is a woman and also expressly includes any less favourable treatment on grounds connected to pregnancy and maternity leave within this heading. There is an important derogation available in the legislation (sections 25 and 27 of the Acts) namely that gender is a bona fide occupational requirement. This exception tends to be strictly interpreted.

Gender discrimination cases tend more frequently to be associated with pregnancy and maternity matters. Equal pay cases still occur but less regularly. There is strong protection afforded to pregnancy and maternity-related issues. An example of this was the case of *O' Brien v. Persian Properties t/a O'Callaghan Hotels* in which the Equality Tribunal (now the WRC) directed an award of EUR 315,000 against the respondent company after finding it had discriminated against the claimant and dismissed them because of their pregnancy. The large award clearly demonstrates the Tribunal's desire to show a deterrent effect in penalizing this type of behaviour.

Harassment is any form of unwanted conduct related to any of the discriminatory grounds listed above. Sexual harassment is any form of unwanted verbal, non-verbal or physical conduct of a sexual nature. The test of whether conduct amounts to harassment is a subjective one ultimately viewed in the eyes/mind of those who suffer the treatment in question. If the conduct has the purpose or effect of violating a person's dignity and creating an intimidating, hostile, degrading, humiliating or offensive environment, then it is considered harassment for which the employer is responsible.

Employers must take all reasonable steps to ensure a workplace is free from harassment and sexual harassment either by preventative or reactive measures.

Employers are vicariously liable for harassment carried out by their employees in the course of their employment, whether the employer knew about the actions complained of or not. The only defence is for an employer to show that it took such steps as were reasonably practicable to prevent such actions. In that regard, Codes of Practice exist to guide employers on what measures or procedures to establish for the prevention of physical and verbal bullying and harassment in the workplace. These include Codes of Practice detailing procedures for addressing bullying in the workplace, Code of Practice on the prevention of workplace bullying and the Code of Practice on Sexual Harassment and Harassment at Work.

There is no statutory requirement for employers to comply with Codes of Practice. It is, however, best practice and compliance undoubtedly strengthens an employer's defence to a claim. It is also good practice for an employer to put in place a specific harassment and bullying prevention policy. The WRC has held that the mere existence of a policy on harassment or an equality policy is not sufficient to prevent discrimination without clearly bringing the provisions of the policy to the attention of staff and creating awareness in all employees as to what constitutes discrimination.[13] Provided that an employer has thoroughly investigated an allegation of harassment and taken appropriate measures to address it, a court is unlikely to find the employer vicariously liable.

13. *Jacqui McCarthy v. Dublin Corporation* [2001] ELR 255.

17.5. Handicap and Disability Discrimination

The definition of disability as set out in the equality legislation is very wide. 'Disability' means:

(1) the total or partial absence of a person's bodily or mental functions, including the absence of a part of a person's body;
(2) the presence in the body of organisms causing, or likely to cause, chronic disease or illness;
(3) the malfunction, malformation or disfigurement of a part of a person's body;
(4) a condition or malfunction which results in a person learning differently from a person without the condition or malfunction; or
(5) a condition, illness or disease which affects a person's thought processes, perception of reality, emotions, judgment or which results in disturbed behaviour, and shall be taken to include a disability which exists at present, or which previously existed but no longer exists or which may exist in the future or which is imputed to a person.

Alcoholism, obsessive compulsive disorder, anorexia, depression and stress have all been held to be disabilities. An employer is not obliged to recruit, train or promote a person who is not fully competent to carry out the duties of a particular job. A person with a disability is considered fully competent to undertake the duties attached to a job if the person could do the duties with the assistance of special treatment or facilities after being reasonably accommodated by the employer. Reasonable accommodation necessitates the taking of appropriate measures by the employer. They include the adaptation of:

(i) premises and equipment;
(ii) patterns of working time;
(iii) the distribution of tasks; or
(iv) the provision of training or integration resources.

They do not include any treatment, facility or thing that the person might ordinarily provide for themselves.

Having determined what facilities and/or special treatment is necessary to make the person fully capable and competent the employer then needs to consider whether the cost of these would impose a 'disproportionate burden' on it.

Factors which may determine whether or not there is a disproportionate burden on the employer include:

(i) the financial and other costs;
(ii) the scale and financial resources of the employer's business;

(iii) the possibility of public funding or other assistance.

An employer should be able to demonstrate that it has investigated the public funding options open to it.

If an employer has followed the above steps they will be better placed to defend an allegation of discrimination on the grounds of disability.

17.6. National Origin Discrimination

This falls under the heading of Race discrimination (*see* above in section 17.3).

17.7. Religious Discrimination

This ground includes within its scope people who are discriminated against on the grounds of religion because of their association with another person or because of their perceived religious belief or none, as with all discrimination grounds.

17.8. Military Status Discrimination

This does not exist in Ireland.

17.9. Pregnancy Discrimination

Ireland has extensive protection for pregnant employees and those that have recently given birth. *See* information under section 17.4 above.

17.10. Marital Status Discrimination

This ground was amended to civil status to take account of changes brought about by the Civil Partnership and Certain Rights and Obligations of Cohabitants Act 2010. The inclusion of civil status means that employers are required to offer the same treatment to civil partners as they would to other employees. As with other grounds, there are exemptions.

17.11. Sexual Orientation Discrimination

In brief this protected ground covers a person's sexual preferences. In order to succeed with a claim a person must show that a person of a different sexual orientation to theirs was treated more favourably than they were. The equality legislation covers imputed discrimination on the grounds of a person's perceived sexual orientation even if the person is not in fact of that orientation.

17.12. Retaliation

The Acts provide protection against victimization. Victimization provides protection for persons from fear or retaliatory action for raising complaints of discrimination with their employer, either as complainants, witnesses or those who assisted parties. In relation to proofs there is no requirement that the claim of discrimination succeeds in order to succeed with a victimization claim. It is a stand-alone cause of action and one in which significant awards have been made in addition to compensation for discriminatory dismissal. The existence of this protection provides a key cornerstone for the fundamental workings of the equality legislation.

17.13. Constructive Discharge

Constructive dismissal arises where an employee is forced to terminate their contract of employment because of the conduct of their employer. Such claims impose a significant burden on employees in order to succeed. Constructive dismissal claims in Ireland are mainly brought under the unfair dismissal regime. There is, however, also a provision to claim discriminatory constructive dismissal under the equality legislation.

17.14. Checklist of Dos and Don'ts

- Ensure that no discrimination takes place at any part of the job lifecycle – i.e., access to jobs, promotion, training and termination of employment.
- Make sure any decisions made in relation to employees are based on objective criteria such as skills and not any underlying impression/motivation.
- Ensure reasonable accommodation is considered where an employee has a disability in the workplace.

18. SMOKING IN THE WORKPLACE

18.1. Overview

Pursuant to the Smoking (Prohibition) Regulations 2003, it is forbidden to smoke in enclosed places of work. This includes office blocks, various buildings, public houses/bars, restaurants and company vehicles (cars and vans).

While smoking in an enclosed workplace is forbidden, employers have discretion to provide an outdoor smoking area, subject to the requirements of the law.

The law has defined an outdoor area as:

- A place or premises, or part of a place or premises that is wholly uncovered by any roof, fixed or mobile.
- An outdoor place or premises that is covered by a roof, so long as not more than 50% of the perimeter (outside) is covered by a wall, windows, gate, or similar.

Any person found guilty of breaching the ban on smoking in the workplace may be subject to a fine. The owner, manager or person in charge of the workplace is legally responsible for ensuring that the ban on smoking in the workplace is complied with.

18.2. Checklist of Dos and Don'ts

- Ensure that smoking is prohibited in the workplace.
- Provide smokers with specially designated outdoor smoking areas.

19. USE OF DRUGS AND ALCOHOL IN THE WORKPLACE

19.1. Overview

The Safety, Health and Welfare at Work Act 2005 is primarily concerned with ensuring insofar as is practicable that the workplace is safe. Section 13 of the Act sets out the general duties of the employer in this regard and identifies the dangers created by an employee under the influence of an intoxicant while at work. Section 13(b) provides that an employee is under a duty to ensure that they are not under the influence of an intoxicant to the extent that they pose a danger to themselves or any other person at work.

Section 13(1)(c) of the 2005 Act provides that an employee must submit to any appropriate, reasonable and proportionate tests for intoxicants by or under the supervision of a medical practitioner. The statutory mechanism for testing employees has not yet been fully implemented although employers can carry out such testing where provision is made in an employee's contract or the business has a specific policy in relation to same or indeed with the express consent of the employee.

19.2. Checklist of Dos and Don'ts

- Given the potential risk and exposure to employers arising out of employees being intoxicated in the workplace (particularly in safety critical roles) and in the absence of statutory authority, employees should have policies in place regarding intoxicants that include testing. Any such policy should be non-discriminatory, proportionate and reasonable.
- Ensure that employees are made aware of the rules on alcohol and drug testing and that the employee is aware of the consequences of breach of those rules.

20. AIDS, HIV, SARS, BLOOD-BORNE PATHOGENS

20.1. Overview

While there is no specific legislation that deals with any of these conditions, section 6(4)(a) of the Unfair Dismissals Act 1977 provides that a dismissal will not be unfair if it arises due to the fact that the employee has been deemed incapable of performing work of a kind for which they had been employed to do. If an employee is absent for a long period due to one of the above conditions, then there may be capability reasons to dismiss. If on the other hand an employee suffers from one of these conditions, they could invoke protection from discrimination on grounds of disability (*see* section 17.5).

20.2. Checklist of Dos and Don'ts

- Do not discriminate against an employee on health grounds as this will be deemed a breach of the Employment Equality Acts 1998–2015.
- Employers should only ask questions relating to an employee's health where it may pose a risk or interfere with the employee's ability to perform the job in question.

21. DRESSING AND GROOMING REQUIREMENTS

21.1. Overview

The enforcement of a dress code will not be discriminatory if it applies a common standard of neatness, conventionality and hygiene to both men and women and does not unreasonably bear more heavily on one gender than it does on the other. A dress code that applies only to one gender (or more onerously to one gender) will be deemed to be discriminatory.

21.2. Checklist of Dos and Don'ts

- If implementing a dress code, ensure that it applies equally to male and female employees.
- Ensure that any dress code implemented does not treat people less favourably in respect of any of the nine protected grounds of discrimination.
- Ensure that any dress code implemented is proportionate and consistent.

22. PRIVACY, TECHNOLOGY AND TRANSFER OF PERSONAL DATA

22.1. Privacy Rights of Employees

The employee's right to privacy may be sourced from the Constitution, the European Convention on Human Rights, the GDPR, data protection legislation (in particular the Data Protection Act 2018) and the contract of employment.

While an employee is entitled to privacy while at work, the right is not unlimited and may be restricted in particular by the rights of others. Thus, an employer may be justified in certain circumstances in breaching an employee's privacy where it is deemed necessary in order to protect the employer's property or business.

Surveillance

While data protection legislation sets out the rights and entitlements of employees regarding the issue of data privacy, the issue of surveillance of electronic communications in the workplace is not specifically legislated for. However, under Article 29 of the European Directive 95/46/EC, a working group of Data Privacy Commissioners produced a Working Document on the issue of surveillance of electronic communications in the workplace. While this document is not legally binding, it would certainly prove to be persuasive.

E-mail and Internet Usage Policy

Employers should provide workers with a readily accessible, clear and accurate statement of policy with regard to e-mail and internet use, including the use of social media, in the workplace. This should clearly describe the extent to which employees can use communication facilities, either owned by the company or personal remote devices such as smartphones, for personal or private communications. For example, the policy may place a limitation on the duration and times of use.

If surveillance or monitoring of communications use is to be carried out, the reasons and purposes for which this will be undertaken must be made clear to employees, especially in light of the GDPR. Where an employer has allowed the use of the company's communication facilities for private use by employees, such private communications may be subject to some surveillance, for example, to ensure adequate virus checking. Details of surveillance measures to be undertaken must be clearly identified, for example, what type of surveillance and how and when it will be done. Employers should ensure employees are fully aware of the surveillance of their private communications to minimize exposure to claims of GDPR breaches.

All these issues should be addressed and included in the employer's policy.

CCTV Surveillance

In Ireland, all usage of CCTV other than in a purely domestic context must be undertaken in compliance with the requirements of data protection legislation. As CCTV infringes the privacy of the persons captured in the images there must be a genuine reason for installing such a system. The use of CCTV surveillance must be transparent.

Employees are entitled to know for what purposes CCTV has been installed and the CCTV footage cannot be used for another purpose.

22.2. Checklist of Dos and Don'ts

- Inform employees if any systems will be put in place for monitoring their activity or personal data.
- If using CCTV surveillance, inform employees of such surveillance, state clearly through signage the whereabouts of such cameras and explain the purpose for which the footage captured by such surveillance is going to be used.

- Inform employees of any sanctions that may be imposed for breaching e-mail and internet usage policies.
- Review all existing policies in respect of surveillance to ensure compliance with the GDPR.

23. WORKPLACE INVESTIGATIONS FOR COMPLAINTS OF DISCRIMINATION, HARASSMENT, FRAUD, THEFT AND WHISTLE-BLOWING

23.1. Overview

In Ireland, employers have a right and a duty to appropriately manage their employees. Appropriate management is a challenging process and there is no such thing as 'one-size-fits-all' rules for each scenario that arises in the workplace. In the event of a dispute arising between an employer and employee, the first step, where this is possible, should be for the parties to engage with each other in an effort to arrive at a suitable resolution on a local and internal level. In this regard, the Government published a Statutory Instrument (S.I. 146 of 2000) entitled the 'Industrial Relations Act, 1990 (Code of Practice on Grievance and Disciplinary Procedures) (Declaration) Order, 2000'.

The main purpose of this Code of Practice is to provide guidance to employers, employees, and their representatives on the general principles which apply in the operation of grievance and disciplinary procedures.

While the Code outlines the principles of fair procedures for employers and employees generally, it is of particular relevance to situations of individual representation.

While arrangements for handling discipline and grievance issues vary considerably from employment to employment depending on a wide variety of factors including the terms of contracts of employment, locally agreed procedures, industry agreements, and whether trade unions are recognized for collective bargaining purposes, the principles, and procedures of this Code of Practice should apply unless alternative agreed procedures exist in the workplace which conform to its general provisions for dealing with grievance and disciplinary issues.

In general, employees are entitled to have allegations or complaints against them properly investigated and dealt with. They should be afforded the right to be represented during any investigative or disciplinary procedure and be given reasonable time and opportunity to prepare and present their response to any such allegations or complaints. Employers should ensure that the employee receives a fair and impartial determination of the issues concerned, taking into account any representations made by them or on their behalf, and any other relevant or appropriate evidence, factors or circumstances.

Employees should also be afforded the opportunity to appeal against any disciplinary action taken against them and to have issues determined by persons who neither have an improper interest in the outcome of the procedure nor might be reasonably apprehended to have such an interest.

23.2. Checklist of Dos and Don'ts

- It is imperative that an employer has the appropriate policies and procedures in place to deal with any complaints of discrimination, fraud, theft and whistle-blowing. These policies should be proactively implemented and training provided for staff to ensure that the employer can point to having taken all reasonable steps to implement the policies in the workplace.
- Efforts should be made, where possible, to resolve the matter internally where possible.
- Under the Protected Disclosures Act 2014 it is an offence to unfairly dismiss an employee for whistle-blowing and the employee may be awarded up to five years' remuneration. Employers should ensure they have appropriate whistle-blowing policies in place designed to meet the requirements of the 2014 Act.

24. AFFIRMATIVE ACTION/NON-DISCRIMINATION REQUIREMENTS

24.1. Overview

The terms affirmative action and positive action are interchangeable terms. There is no formal legal definition; however, they are generally taken to mean the promotion of actions that achieve non-discrimination. An example of positive action is the provision of special training courses for women who are underrepresented in a specific skill area. It is often used in government and education settings to ensure minority groups are represented within society. Under EU law positive action is allowed; however, positive discrimination is not. The Employment Equality Acts 1998–2015 do allow for positive action to be taken as a means of ensuring full equality between men and women in practice. The adoption and maintenance of measures to prevent or compensate for disadvantages linked to a discriminatory ground (other than gender), or to protect the health and safety of workers with a disability, also are permitted.

24.2. Checklist of Dos and Don'ts

– Ensure any measures designed to address inequalities in the workplace are reviewed regularly as the business needs evolve and change.

25. RESOLUTION OF LABOUR, DISCRIMINATION AND EMPLOYMENT DISPUTES: LITIGATION, ARBITRATION, MEDIATION AND CONCILIATION

25.1. Internal Dispute Resolution Process

Employees are entitled to be made aware of both the existence and content of the disciplinary rules in operation in the organization, and should they be the subject of a disciplinary investigation, of all aspects of that investigation and of the charges that they are facing, not least so that they can properly defend themselves.

25.2. Mediation and Conciliation

The Mediation Act 2017 came into law on 1 January 2018. This Act places a statutory obligation on litigants to consider mediation and requires litigants to confirm to the Courts that they have considered mediation. The significant majority of employment-related disputes are exempt from this requirement. However, mediation in this context is provided for under the Workplace Relations Act 2015.

The Workplace Relations Act places a significant emphasis on mediation and resolving disputes as close to the workplace as possible. When a complaint arrives at the WRC it may be referred to a mediation officer if it is deemed suitable for early resolution. If so, and if both parties agree to it, then a mediation conference (potentially held over the phone) will be convened. Any resolution arising from this will be binding on the parties and enforceable in the Courts.

If early resolution is not deemed appropriate, is refused by the parties or if an attempted mediation is unsuccessful, a dispute will be referred to a single adjudicator at the WRC.

25.3. Arbitration

Arbitration is an alternative way of resolving any type of dispute. The arbitrator hears the disagreement between one or more parties and after considering all relevant information renders a final decision in favour of one of the parties. Decisions may be binding or non-binding, depending on the terms of the arbitration agreement. While employment disputes may be arbitrated, they are not covered by the Arbitration Act 2010 and therefore do not have the same legal protection.

25.4. Litigation

The Workplace Relations Act 2015 provides for all appeals to the Labour Court, and it acts as a court of final appeal for all adjudication decisions of the WRC. There is an appeal only on a point of law to the High Court.

The Labour Court Rules detail the process associated with appealing a decision of an Adjudication Officer of the WRC.

Another prominent area of litigation which has come to the force in recent years is that of the Employment Injunction. This is a form of relief that may be sought by either an employee or an employer (though in most cases it is sought by the employee) and, if granted, will have the effect of requiring the party against whom it is granted either to do or to refrain from doing something, or both.

The four most common types of relief sought by employees applying for an injunction against their employer are:

(1) an order reinstating the employee who has been dismissed to their former position;
(2) an order restraining the dismissal of an employee (but not requiring their reinstatement), which essentially means that the employer is bound to pay the employee for the duration of the order;
(3) an order restraining the employer from taking steps to compromise the position of the employee within the business, such as appointing a replacement or reorganizing the business;
(4) an order requiring that disciplinary hearings be conducted in accordance with fair procedures.

25.5. Fines, Penalties and Damages

Fines, penalties and damages will vary depending on the facts and before what authority the case is heard. The WRC can award compensation of up to two years' gross remuneration, reinstatement or re-engagement where an employee has been dismissed. The WRC, in addition to the remedies above, can also order the employer to take a specified cause of action under the employment equality legislation.

25.6. Checklist of Dos and Don'ts

– Depending on the circumstances, it may be advisable to try to resolve disputes informally through alternative dispute resolution procedures rather than resorting to court proceedings which are more costly and time-consuming.

26. EMPLOYER RECORDKEEPING, DATA PROTECTION AND EMPLOYEE ACCESS TO PERSONNEL FILES, AND RECORDS

26.1. Overview

The EU GDPR and the Data Protection Act 2018 introduce substantial changes to data protection law which impact the employer/employee relationship.

One significant area that has been impacted is reliance by the employer on the employee's consent to process their data. It was a common practice for employment contracts to include a blanket consent provision under the heading 'data protection'. Typically this provided that the employee consents to the use and processing of their data under the contract (e.g., transfer of personal data overseas, monitoring, disclosure of sensitive personal data to third parties and the sharing of information with a wide variety of partners for payroll, insurance and health-related purposes). It is unlikely that this form of consent is effective in the GDPR era and, even if it is, under GDPR employees have a right to withdraw their consent at any time.

If an employer wishes to continue to rely on 'consent' as a basis for processing employees' personal data, any such consent should be separate from the employment contract. Employees should also be expressly advised of their right to withdraw consent at any time and it must be easy for them to do so.

Many employers will seek an alternative legal basis for processing. The following legal bases are provided for under the GDPR:

(1) Where the processing is necessary for the performance of the contract with the employer or to enter into such a contract.
(2) Where the processing is necessary for compliance with a legal obligation to which the employer is subject.
(3) Where the processing is necessary to protect the vital interests of the employee or another person.
(4) Where the processing is necessary for the performance of a task carried out in the public interest.

(5) Where the processing is necessary for the purposes of the legitimate interests of the employer or a third party except where such interests are overridden by the interests of the employee.
(6) Where the processing is necessary for the purposes of the legitimate interests of the employer or a third party except where such interests are overridden by the interests of the employee.

Where consent is relied on as a ground for processing sensitive personal data (e.g., religious beliefs, health data, sexual orientation, trade union membership), the GDPR requires such consent to be explicit – i.e., clear, specific and unambiguous.

The GDPR provides for significant sanctions in situations of non-compliance by employers. Maximum fines include up to EUR 20 million or 4% of global turnover.

Privacy Notices

The GDPR requires employers to provide employees (data subjects) with the following information by way of a 'Privacy Notice':

(1) The identity and contact details of the employer/its representative.
(2) The contact details of the data protection officer (if applicable).
(3) The purpose of the processing and the legal basis for the processing.
(4) The legitimate interests of the employer/third party and an explanation of those interests.
(5) The recipients or categories of recipients of the personal data.
(6) Details of any transfers out of the EEA, safeguards in place and the means by which to obtain a copy of them.

In addition to the above, employers are required, to ensure the processing is fair and transparent, to provide the following information:

(1) The data retention period or criteria to determine same.
(2) The employees' rights, including the right of access to data; rectification and erasure; restriction of the processing; objection to the processing and to data portability.
(3) Where the processing is based on consent, the right to withdraw consent at any time.
(4) The right to complain to the supervisory authority (the Data Protection Commission (DPC)).
(5) Details of automated decision-making, including profiling and logic involved, as well as the significance and consequences of such processing for the employee.
(6) Whether the provision of personal data is a statutory or contractual requirement or obligation, and the consequences of failure to provide such data.

Data Subject Access Requests

Since 25 May 2018, employers are required to respond to DSARs within one calendar month. This can be extended by a further two months where requests are complex or numerous and the employee is informed of the proposed extension within a month of the employer's receipt of the DSAR.

Employees are not required to pay any fee for the employer's response to a DSAR (except where the DSAR is clearly unfounded or excessive).

Security Obligations

The GDPR increases employer obligations to protect the security and integrity of personal data. Data must be protected by appropriate technical and organizational measures. In particular, employers must consider the risks presented by accidental or unlawful destruction, loss, alteration, unauthorized disclosure of, or access to personal data transmitted, stored or otherwise processed.

Appropriate technical and organizational measures include:

(1) Pseudonymization.
(2) The ability to ensure ongoing confidentiality, integrity, availability and resilience of processing systems and services.
(3) The ability to restore the availability and access to personal data in a timely manner in the event of a physical or technical incident.
(4) A process for regularly testing, accessing and evaluating the effectiveness of technical and organizational measures to ensure the security of the processing.

Retention

Employers are bound under a host of statutory provisions to maintain a variety of records in relation to employees and their employment. Employers must keep records to demonstrate compliance with the following key legislative provisions:

- Terms of Employment (Information) Acts 1994–2014.
- Organisation of Working Time Act 1997.
- Payment of Wages Act 1991.
- National Minimum Wage Act 2000 and 2015.
- Protection of Employees (Young Persons) Act 1996.
- Parental Leave Acts 1998–2019.
- Carer's Leave Act 2001.
- Industrial Relations Acts 1946–2015.
- Protection of Employment Acts 1977–2014.

26.2. Confidentiality Rules

Employees have a right to obtain a copy of any information relating to them kept on a computer or in a structured manual filing system by any person or organization, regardless of when the data was created. This is done via an access request. Personnel records can be requested such as information relating to disciplinary/grievance issues, appraisal and performance, and medical reports. The general rule is that an employee is entitled to access personal data relating to them in connection with discipline/grievance issues subject to certain exceptions. Those exceptions relate to: (i) opinions given in confidence; (ii) professional legal privilege; (iii) protecting the source of the data; (iv) investigation of an offence, and exemptions relating to back up data and estimates of liability in relation to a claim for compensation. The most relevant here are opinions given in confidence or on the understanding that it would be treated as confidential. This test must satisfy a high threshold of confidentiality. Merely putting the word ‘confidential’ at the top of the document will not automatically render it confidential. The Data Protection Commissioner will look at the data and its context and will need to be satisfied that the data would not otherwise have been given but for this understanding.

27. REQUIRED NOTICES AND POSTINGS

27.1. Overview

Pursuant to relevant legislation, an employer must display certain information in the workplace, including the following.

Under the Safety, Health and Welfare at Work Act, 2005, an employer must bring the safety statement to the attention of their existing employees at least annually, to any new employees upon commencement of their employment and other persons at the place of work who may be exposed to any specific risk. They are also required to keep a copy or relevant extract of the safety statement available for inspection at or near every place of work to which it relates while work is being carried out. Also, when an improvement notice is served, the person to whom it is addressed shall display the notice or a copy of the notice in a prominent place at or near any place of work, article or substance affected by the notice.

The Public Health (Tobacco) Act 2002 requires that at all times a sign be displayed to indicate areas where smoking is permitted and areas where smoking is not permitted. The sign should also display the name of the occupier of the premises and the name of the person to whom a complaint may be made by a member of the public.

Under the Protection of Young Persons (Employment) Act, 1996, every employer who has employees under the age of 18 must display the official summary (abstract) of the Act at the workplace where it can be easily read.

27.2. Checklist of Dos and Don'ts

- Where required by legislation, every employer should ensure that all notices are displayed in a prominent and accessible part of the premises.

www.ingramcontent.com/pod-product-compliance
Ingram Content Group UK Ltd.
Pitfield, Milton Keynes, MK11 3LW, UK
UKHW020150290926
15471UKWH00004B/796

9 789403 503264